JOHANN SEBASTIAN BACH

(*woodcut by Eric King*)

BACH

by ESTHER MEYNELL

Great Lives

DUCKWORTH
3 HENRIETTA STREET
LONDON   W.C.2

First published 1934
Reprinted 1946, 1949, 1962

Printed in Great Britain
by Gilmour & Dean Ltd., Glasgow and London

To

DR. C. SANFORD TERRY

whose name is inseparably linked with
Johann Sebastian Bach
this small book

CONTENTS

CONTENTS

CHRONOLOGY

1685....Bach born at Eisenach, March 21.

1695....Left an orphan.

1700....Goes to Convent School at Lüneburg.

1703....Becomes organist at Arnstadt.

1704....His first church cantata performed.

1705....Goes to Lübeck to hear Buxtehude.

1707....Becomes organist at Mühlhausen.

1707....Marries his cousin Maria Barbara Bach.

1708....Appointed Court Organist at Weimar.

1717....Becomes *Capellmeister* at Cöthen.

1720....His wife dies

1721....Marries Anna Magdalena Wilcken.

1723....Appointed Cantor of the Leipzig
        Thomasschule.

1729....*Matthäuspassion.*

1733....Mass in B minor.

1736....*Hof-Compositeur* to the Court of Dresden.

1747....Visits Frederick the Great at Potsdam.

1750....Dies at Leipzig, July 28.

CHAPTER I

Death of a cantor—birth of Bach—his forebears—early years—
his scores—goes to Lüneburg—organ journeys—" I worked
hard."

IN the year 1750, in the month of July, there died
in a German provincial town, a German composer and organist, cantor of a boys' school, of
some local fame, but with a name hardly known
outside Saxony. He died and was buried. His
fellow-townsmen, who had found him in certain
matters a little difficult and stubborn, expressed
a moderate regret at his decease, promptly forgot
him with all decent speed, and turned to the
consideration of their own important affairs.

A few pupils of the dead musician—mostly
organists and cantors in small Thuringian towns
—still cherished his memory and played his compositions. One or two of them even exhibited
a kind of idolatry towards him, like Johann
Philipp Kirnberger, who hung his master's
portrait in his room in Berlin in order that he
might gaze upon it daily with reverent affection.
The story is told of him that on one occasion he
was visited by a wealthy Leipzig linen-merchant.
Scarcely had this visitor sat down when he
beheld the portrait, and exclaimed, " Good

11

Lord ! I see you have our cantor hanging there ; we have him also in Leipzig in the Thomasschule. He was a rough fellow—if the vain fool has not had himself painted in a splendid velvet coat ! " Whereupon Kirnberger jumped up, and, seizing him by the collar, ran the astonished merchant from the room, exclaiming, " Out, dog ! Out, dog ! "

Another pupil, Christian Kittel, kept his master's portrait above his organ, as in a shrine, hidden from the gaze of the profane by a curtain, and only allowed the favoured few to look upon it. Of course it was obvious from their curious behaviour that these people were a little mad, and in time death shut their mouths, and then Germany comfortably forgot that such a person as Johann Sebastian Bach had ever existed— forgot so completely that the Leipzig Town Council turned the churchyard of the Johan- niskirche where he was buried to secular uses and obliterated the very place of his grave.

There was a real German thoroughness about their methods.

Then, nearly eighty years after Bach's death, it fell to the lot of a happy and fortunate German musician, who deserved his name of Felix— Felix Mendelssohn Bartholdy—to conduct the first performance of the *Matthäuspassion*, the first performance, that is, since it had been done under Bach's own direction exactly a century earlier. Then musicians began to wonder why Bach's music had been so strangely forgotten.

.   .   .   .

Sebastian Bach was born in the spring of 1685 —the day he entered the world was a Saturday, March 21—at Eisenach in Thuringia, a place set amidst woods and waters, in sight of the Wartburg, full of romantic historical associations and of natural beauty. German song and Luther's translation of the Bible were associated there. In the streets of Eisenach, where the young Sebastian was to take his first steps, Luther, two centuries earlier, had wandered singing from door to door. Eisenach was a fitting place for the birth of Johann Sebastian Bach. The long, low, red-roofed house there, which is now a Bach Museum, and was for many years believed to be his birthplace, has, owing to recent research, been deposed from that honour. His father, Johann Ambrosius Bach, was a householder in the Fleischgasse—now the Lutherstrasse—from 1679 till the time of his death, and it is, therefore, highly improbable that Johann Sebastian was not born under his father's roof. But, under whatever roof, there could be little doubt that, born of such parentage, he was destined to become a musician. His father was a musician, his elder brother was a musician, so were his uncles and cousins. The Bachs had music in their blood.

Of some sixty members of the family through
several generations whose names and professions
are on record, all save seven were organists,
cantors, or "town musicians." In Erfurt,
musicians were known as "the Bachs" even
when they bore a quite different family name—
Bach had come to mean musician. Even if they
ground corn for a living, as did Sebastian's great-
great-grandfather, Veit Bach, in the sixteenth
century, they still must comfort themselves with
music. Sebastian himself has recorded how old
Veit Bach took the greatest delight in his lute,
which it was his habit to carry with him into the
mill and play while the grain was being ground
into flour. "A pretty noise the pair of them
must have made!" he remarks, and somewhat
quaintly adds, "However, it taught him to keep
time."

Into the long and honourable musical records
of the Bach family it is impossible to enter here.
It is a remarkable and interesting story, and those
who wish may find full particulars in the pon-
derously enthralling volumes of Philipp Spitta,
and will, after doing so, not only be convinced of
the musicianly inheritance of the Bachs, but will
agree with Spitta that they were "a race of the
greatest health and vigour, a family of the soundest
morality."

The small Sebastian showed the same interest
in, and attachment to, music as his forebears,

but there was nothing of the prodigy about him, nothing to suggest how tremendously beyond the stature of those forebears he was to grow. Abnormal in his gifts, there was nothing abnormal in his character—throughout the records of his life he leaves an impression of sanity, balance, wisdom. He is like a great tree, his boughs waving high among the stars, while his roots are embedded deeply and securely in the wholesome earth.

He was early left to grow on his own roots, as it were, and this undoubtedly helped to establish that sturdy independence of character which belonged to him. His father, Johann Ambrosius Bach, who was an accomplished violin and viola player and had taught these instruments to his youngest son, died before Sebastian had reached the age of ten. His mother also had died only a few months previously. This caused a shifting of the family of growing children. One of Sebastian's sisters was about to be married to Andreas Wiegand of Erfurt—Eisenach, Erfurt, and Arnstadt were special abodes of the Bach clans. An older brother, Johann Christoph, himself recently married, was residing at Ohrdruf, and to his care went the two young boys, Jakob, aged thirteen, and Sebastian, within a month of ten years old. This was in February 1695. Four years later, Sebastian was confirmed, and when he was within a few days of his fifteenth birthday he relieved his brother of the necessity of his support, and began thus early industriously to earn his own living, as he was to do for the next fifty years, with no assistance from the gifts of fortune, just by plain hard work. His genius brought neither riches nor great fame to his life. As an executant musician he became something of a celebrity in a narrow circle—as a composer few people of his day recognised him as anything more than competent.

He had begun his general education at the gymnasium at Eisenach, where he learned the Catechism, Psalter, and Latin. At Ohrdruf he entered the Lyceum, and very rapidly and steadily earned promotion in his classes. " His class record," says Dr. Sanford Terry, " shows him exceptionally quick-witted and informed : he was barely fifteen when he passed out of Prima, a class in which, while he was at school, the average age was never less than seventeen." It is evident he had a good sound brain, combined with habits of application, apart from his musical abilities. He also had an *ungemein schöne Sopranstimme*, and sang in both school and church. His brother, who himself had been a pupil of Pachelbel, gave him systematic teaching on the clavier, and to this period of his life belongs one of the few personal stories his biography bestows upon us. His elder brother apparently endeavoured to confine him to the simple pieces he considered suitable to the pupil's age. But Sebastian's

abilities and ambitions ranged ahead of his
teacher, and he particularly set his heart on a
collection of manuscript music by the famous
composers of that period, such as Froberger,
Fischer, Pachelbel, Kerll, Buxtehude. Appeals
to be allowed to study this music were refused :
even to handle it was apparently forbidden, for
the manuscript was caged behind the lattice-
work of a locked cupboard. But the need and
desire for knowledge in young Sebastian over-
came the stupid prohibition. For the moonlight
nights of six months he sat up secretly at the
window of his little bed-chamber and patiently
copied out the music which he had managed to
abstract through the bars of the cupboard—he
had to do this on moonlight nights, as the economi-
cal household allowed him no candle. It shows
the extraordinary tenacity and purpose of this
child, for he was little more, to continue such a
task for six months. But when the long labour
was at length finished, his brother discovered
what he had done, and, with a curious disci-
plinary harshness, confiscated the fruit of so
much toil. But he could not take away from the
young Sebastian the knowledge that had passed into his receptive brain as he copied out that music.

All his life it was a habit of Bach's to copy out
with painstaking care the music of other composers. " He absorbed all styles," says Cecil
Gray in his *History of Music*, " instead of being

Bʙ

absorbed by them." He was willing to learn
to the day of his death, and displayed in later
years an admiration for, and interest in, the music
of Handel, which Handel, apparently, did not
take in his.

This constant copying of music, apart from
the writing of vast quantities of his own, had a
most deleterious effect on his eyesight—but even
that must be sacrificed to the getting of knowledge.
His portraits show what this close application
had done to his eyes. In Jakob Ihle's portrait
in the Bach Museum at Eisenach, showing Sebastian when he was thirty-five, his eyes are large
and strong in their gaze ; in the Haussmann
portrait of twenty-six years later, the eyes have
narrowed, the brows are drawn down in the
effort of protecting and focusing the sight. And
at the end of his life he was actually blind.
Probably few human pursuits are worse for the
eyes than the constant writing of music. And in
those days the staves had to be ruled, as well as
the actual notes written. To look at some of
Bach's manuscripts in facsimile, such as the
magnificent reproduction of the *Matthäuspassion*
by the Insel-Verlag, or at the actual script of
Bach's own hand, as in the second volume of the
" 48 Preludes and Fugues," which is one of the
greatest treasures of the British Museum, is to
come very close to the composer. One sees the
irregular ruling of the lines, where they were

not quite long enough, or the ruler did not
reach across the page and a fresh start was made ;
there are places where a thread or a speck of
dust thickened the pen ; there are vigorous
scorings out ; there are notes splashed in with
an over-full quill ; and in blank corners of some
of the manuscripts he has written down hurriedly,
catching his thought on the wing, a theme for
some other work which has come to him while
he was engaged on the music under his hand.
It is like being privileged to bend over Bach's
shoulder and watch with amazement the creation
of immortal music.

When the boy who later was to write these
things left his brother's roof and went to Lüneburg
where he entered the choir of St. Michael's
Convent, he no longer had to obtain his music
in secrecy and by the light of the moon, for he
had the unrestricted use of the music in the richly
stored Convent library, which was so wide in its
range as to include music of the time of Luther,
and motets of Sebastian's own relations Heinrich
and Johann Christoph Bach—the latter at that
time still alive. It is easy to imagine what this
wide selection of music meant to the boy whose
opportunities had hitherto been so limited. The
records of his life prove that it was as impossible
for Sebastian to be near music and not use and
profit by it as it would be unnatural for a duck
to be near water and not swim in it.

Soon after he entered the choir his voice broke
—he is known to have possessed a soprano voice
of a seraphic quality, and, when it broke, a
curious thing happened to him : he found that
he had, as it were, a double voice, that he both
sang and spoke in octaves. This effect lasted
for a week. But Sebastian very literally had other
strings to his bow than his voice. If that failed
him, he could take up his violin or viola and
earn his keep as an accompanist. At Lüneburg
he received instruction on the organ, from the
organist of the Johanniskirche, Georg Böhm, a
Thuringian like himself. Böhm had been a pupil
of Reinken, and no doubt his talk of his old
master filled Sebastian with the desire to hear
him, and on foot he set out to walk the thirty
miles across the barren Lüneburger Heath to
Hamburg to satisfy his desire to hear that notable
organist. Mizler said that " he was moved by
a particularly strong impulse that he should hear
as many good organists as possible."

It is a picture that pleases the imagination,
this boy, poor, unknown, bearing a name so
common in his own part of Germany, setting
out on these humble expeditions. There were
so many Johanns among the Bach clans that it
was entirely necessary to have a second name to
distinguish them one from another. It is a
curious fact that, though among the names which
marked out the Johanns from each other there

are names as uncommon as Ambrosius and Egidius, there is only the one Sebastian in the recorded names up to Johann Sebastian's own birth. He owed this name to the second of his godfathers, Sebastian Nagel. Among his own sons there is none bearing that name, and of two grandsons who in his honour were christened after him one died in infancy and one as a young man. It was as though destiny meant his name, like his genius, to stand apart. So this young Johann Sebastian, with no consciousness of the weight and significance of the name he bore, set out upon his travels, walking many lengthy miles, arriving dusty and tired at some church, leaning against a wall, or sitting on some bench to listen. Modesty or shyness seems to have prevented him from making himself known to the organists hc came to hear—at least in these early visits. He listened and walked away again, unknown and unnoticed, bearing in his brain those seeds which were to flower so gloriously in later years into Choral Preludes, into Toccatas and Fugues, into the garnered sweetness of the " Little Book for the Organ."

As he had but few groschen in his pocket, Sebastian often went hungry as well as footsore, and he himself told the story to Marpurg—who published it thirty-six years after Bach's death— of how on one occasion fortune came to aid his need. He had been to Hamburg to listen to

Adam Reinken, and he came to an inn outside which he sat down to rest, hungry, but too poor to pay for a meal, though his hunger was naturally increased by the pleasant odours proceeding from the kitchen. Suddenly a window was flung open and two herrings' heads were thrown out. That was not much of a meal, but young Sebastian was hungry enough to pick them up, and found, to his surprise, inside each head a Danish ducat. It sounds exactly like a story of Hans Andersen, but it is true on Bach's own authority. It not only gave him the good meal of which he stood in need, but, characteristically, he used the money to return again to Hamburg and hear some more organ music. For that food, he was eternally hungry.

The organ, by its nature polyphonic, was, before all others, his instrument. To take away the organ would be to take away the heart of his musical life, both as performer and composer. Events and compositions to be detailed later will show the basis of this statement. As his brother was organist at Ohrdruf, it was there, in all probability, that he first made intimate acquaintance with his destined instrument. When he went to Lüneburg, he turned his face to a region of great organists—Adam Reinken at Hamburg, Dietrich Buxtehude at Lübeck, as well as Georg Böhm at Lüneburg itself. But Sebastian at this time listened not only to organists—on occasion

he turned his footsteps to Celle, where, at the
Court of Duke George Wilhelm, he heard the
newest and gayest of French music, and where
dresses and manners alike were modelled on the
elegancies of Versailles. Deep and solid German
as Sebastian was born, he would yet not pass by
the excellencies and charms of French and Italian
music when it came his way. To him music was
a country that had no frontiers, wherever melody
breathed he was at home. In later years he
showed appreciation of Couperin, and copied into
the *Notenböchlein* he made for his wife Anna
Magdalena in 1725 a rondeau by him. In this
earlier time he copied out two suites, in A major
and F minor, by French composers, and a table
of " ornaments " in the French manner, which
were not then in general use in Germany, with
directions as to playing them. In that great
work of his later years the *Kunst der Fuge* the sixth
counterpoint is marked " In the French style."
From a French composer, André Raison, he
took the subject of his noble Passacaglia for the
organ. Many other instances could be given of
the effect of the " French style " upon his
markedly German mentality. Well was he
entitled to say to one who asked his secret, " I
worked hard." Hard work, more than kind
fortune or unusual opportunities, was always at
the root of his achievement. His nature had the
rare combination of flexibility with strength. At

different times in his life he was placed in positions where it was necessary that he should compose music of a particular description—for the organ, for voices, chamber music, or church cantatas. He did this to the full of his powers, never apparently grudging or grieving that one kind of music was demanded above another. He was always limited and handicapped by the resources he had at his disposal, especially during the long years at Leipzig—imperfect choirs, unbalanced orchestras, with defective instruments, and players of the most moderate skill, or even immoderate incompetence. For such choirs and such orchestras he wrote the music that yet has such eternal quality that no musician can even imagine the day when Bach shall be outmoded and passed by.

CHAPTER II

WHEN he was eighteen years old, Bach received an appointment which gave him an organ of his own. With that appointment he may be said to have grown up. He became organist at the Bonifaciuskirche at Arnstadt, where there was a newly built and just completed organ he had been requested to examine and report upon—this was the first of many such commissions, and shows how early his remarkable abilities in regard to the organ showed themselves. He was also requested to inaugurate the new Arnstadt organ by a public performance the Sunday after the examination was completed. His playing so impressed the Consistorium that they immediately offered him the post of organist, which he accepted and was confirmed in on August 9, 1703. For pay he was to have fifty florins a year, with thirty thalers for board and lodging. For this sum he was to " eschew other tasks and occupations," he was to " attend at the organ " and " perform thereon as shall be required " ; in his conduct and behaviour he was to be " God-fearing, temperate, well-disposed to all folk."

Before he obtained this appointment, Sebastian had applied for the post of organist at a church in Sangerhausen, and obtained it on his merits ; but he was put aside on the score of his youth, and an organist eleven years older was inducted instead. He had also been, for a short time, in the employ of the younger brother of the Duke of Weimar, but this was only a passing episode, though later on he was to return to Weimar.

It may easily be imagined that for his Arnstadt organ Sebastian had a peculiar affection. It comprised a Pedal Organ of five speaking stops, with a coupler to the manuals ; a Great Organ (*Oberwerk*) of twelve stops, and *Brustwerk*—corresponding to the Swell Organ, only not having its pipes enclosed in a swell-box—of nine stops, with a coupler to the Great. The manuals, pedals, and stop handles of this instrument, in their plain original case, are still preserved in the Arnstadt Museum.[1]

The principles of organ-playing were the same in Bach's day as they are now, the legato organ touch as necessary, as the sound ceases if the finger leaves the key. But the technical difficulties were much greater, as the keys were stiff, often needing physical strength to depress them ; the stops were heavy and hard to pull out ; the pedal keys too short to allow the use of the heel

[1] The full specification is to be found in Dr. Sanford Terry's *Bach : a Biography.*

as well as the toe. The wind was supplied by
" treading " the bellows. All his life, Bach was
interested in the structural improvement of
organs, of whose construction he had a technical
knowledge—it is evident he had a natural genius
not only for the playing but for the building of
instruments, both of keyed and stringed kinds,
of which in his later years he planned several
varieties, as well as advising Silbermann in the
construction of his " hammerclaviers." The
technical difficulties that he had to surmount
render his performances on the organ, which
later excited so much admiration, the more
wonderful.

. Coupled with his duties at the organ in Arnstadt
was the less agreeable one of training the choir,
composed of a particularly unruly lot of boys.
All his life, Bach seems to have found difficulty
in dealing with boys in the mass, as many episodes
in his cantorship at Leipzig show. To his private
and personal pupils he exhibited qualities that
produced a devotion approaching adoration, and
he instilled into them the finest ideals of musicianship. But a set of undisciplined boys was an
instrument upon which he could not play : unlike
his " Well-tempered Clavier " it was not responsive to his touch.

While at Arnstadt, Sebastian began not only
" assiduously to study the works of the celebrated
organists of his period," as Forkel tells us, but to

compose works of his own. To this period of his life belongs the delightful Capriccio in B flat he wrote on the " Departure of a Beloved Brother " —this brother being Johann Jakob, who had entered the service of King Charles XII of Sweden as oboist. Before starting, he visited both Ohrdruf and Arnstadt to say farewell to Johann Christoph and Johann Sebastian, and the latter wrote for the occasion his delicate and descriptive little composition, which Sir Hubert Parry calls " the most dextrous piece of work of the kind that had ever appeared in the world up to that time."

He also wrote another Capriccio in honour of his Ohrdruf brother. And to this period belongs, in the opinion of Dr. Sanford Terry, " the earliest example of Bach's genius in the cantata form, eloquent of the northern influences to which Lüneburg had exposed him." He composed as well the Sonata in D major, the Organ Prelude and Fugue in C minor, and another Organ Fugue in the same key. He was gathering in experience and knowledge with eager hands. His zeal to increase them both provides us with another of the scanty personal glimpses that the records reveal.

The " Evening Music " at the Marienkirche in Lübeck, under the direction of Buxtehude, was famous. It took place after Vespers, about four o'clock, on three Sundays of Advent. Sebastian wanted to hear this music. Lübeck, it is

true, was a distance of three hundred miles from
Arnstadt, but that distance was no obstacle to
his ardour. It is stated by his earliest biographers
that he covered it on foot, but it seems at least
probable that he would get lifts by the way, even
if his frugal mind did not allow him to hire
any means of conveyance. His cousin Johann
Ernst was in Arnstadt at this time, and Sebastian,
being able to offer him as a substitute at his
organ, obtained leave to be absent a month so
that he might visit Lübeck and hear the " Evening
Music " which so attracted him. He left Arnstadt
in October 1705 : he returned in January 1706.
The authorities were naturally surprised and
annoyed at the cool behaviour of their young
organist. He was, as the records tell, " summoned
to explain his prolonged absence and discon-
tinuance of figural music." The following
conversation took place, which is here given
in Dr. Sanford Terry's vivid translation. The
Superintendent of the Consistorium, Johann
Christoph Olearius, presided, and questioned
Bach.

Olearius : " The Consistorium desires to know
where you have been for so long, and who gave
you leave of absence.

Bach : " I have been to Lübeck to study my
profession, and before I went, Herr Superintendent, I asked your permission.

Olearius : " That is so ; but you said you would

be away four weeks and have been absent four months. What explanation do you offer ?

Bach : " I thought my deputy would satisfactorily fill my place, and consequently that no complaint would be made.

Olearius : " Complaints have been made to the Consistorium that you now accompany the hymns with surprising variations and irrelevant ornaments, which obliterate the melody and confuse the congregation. If you desire to introduce a theme against the melody, you must go on with it and not immediately fly off to another. And in no circumstances must you introduce a *tonus contrarius*.

" There is another matter : we are surprised that you have given up performing figural music, and conclude that the omission is due to your bad relations with the pupils of the gymnasium. We must therefore ask you to tell us explicitly that you are prepared to practise them in figural music as well as in the hymns. We cannot provide a cantor, and you must tell us categorically, yes or no, whether you will do what we require. If you will not, we must find an organist who will."

Bach repeated the demand he had made on an earlier occasion for a " Director Musices " for the choir (when he made this demand he received the reproof that " Man lebe mit *imperfectis* ") and nothing more was to be got out of him. We have an amusing little sidelight on his temper in the statement that he " used to play too long preludes, but after this was notified to him by the Herr Superintendent, he went at once quite to the opposite extreme and has made them too short."

We feel the quiet obstinacy, which was one of the Bach characteristics, and are conscious of the somewhat irritable scorn felt by the brilliant young organist at the interference and scolding— mild though it must be admitted to be—of what to him were a set of old greybeards. We feel in his answers some of the haughtiness of genius— though never was genius more balanced and less " temperamental " than Bach's. Glorious vistas were opening to his mind, he was full of all he had heard and learned from the great Buxtehude at Lübeck, he must have felt himself cramped by the conditions and disagreements of Arnstadt.

There was in him a quiet determination to get what he wanted in his own way. Arnstadt was ceasing to suit his need. He had plainly a great admiration for Buxtehude, and perhaps he might have had the reversion of Buxtehude's post, a post that was important and remunerative. There was at this time in Germany a somewhat quaint custom of the organist handing on his position to a son-in-law—the young man who wished to sit on the organ-stool of a particular church married the retiring organist's daughter, and the thing was done. Buxtehude himself had done

this, and Heinrich Bach at Arnstadt had handed
over his daughter as well as his organ to his
successor Christoph Herthum. Buxtehude also
had a daughter, and in 1703, two young men,
George Friederich Handel and Johann Mattheson,
had journeyed to Lübeck with the idea that one
of them might marry Anna Margreta Buxtehude
and become organist at the Marienkirche. But,
unfortunately, Anna Margreta's attractions were
fewer than her years, as she was approaching
thirty, and the two young men walked away
again. Then, a little later, Sebastian Bach
appeared, but he was no more inclined than
Handel to take a fine musical position that
carried with it a compulsory wife. Possibly his
heart was not free. It can safely be assumed that
he would choose his wife for himself, and obtain
his organ in another way.

On his return from Lübeck to Arnstadt there
was another subject of which the Consistory
complained, and in it we find certain elucidations
of a very personal matter. It was stated when he
was again called before the Consistorium and
reproved for his neglect of rehearsing his choir,
that he had admitted a *fremde Jungfer* to his
organ gallery when he was practising, and that
her voice had been heard singing there. This
"stranger maiden" was actually Sebastian's
cousin, Maria Barbara Bach, daughter of the
gifted Michael Bach of Gehren, her mother

belonging to Arnstadt. In a little under a year from the time of this inquisition, Sebastian was to marry her, so no doubt young love was coming to bloom in that organ-loft, and added a further wonder to the music pouring from those organ pipes and from the throat of a girl who gazed at Sebastian's face and saw there, in her clairvoyante state, all his yet unfolded genius. Maria Barbara, coming as she did of the same musical stock as Sebastian, was fitted by nature to appreciate and understand his musicianship. It is evident that her visits to the church to listen to Sebastian's practising were fairly frequent, for he had spoken to the Prediger about the matter before the Consistorium began to interfere.

No doubt this interference affected him unpleasantly at a very sensitive moment of his life, and circumstances helped his desire to move to another place, where he hoped to find conditions nearer to his wishes. Owing to the death of its organist, he was offered the post in the Kirche Divi Blasii at Mühlhausen. He accepted this offer, and arrived there on June 14, 1707, to discuss the terms that he wished to receive, which resolved themselves into 85 gulden in money, with " 3 measures of corn, 2 trusses of wood, one of beech, one of oak or aspen, and 6 trusses of faggots, delivered at his door, in lieu of arable." He also requested a wagon in which to convey his possessions from Arnstadt to Mühlhausen. The

Cʙ

town of his new abode must have looked strangely
desolate on that June day to Sebastian's eyes, for
at the end of May it had been ravaged by a
fearful fire in which four hundred houses were
destroyed, and the Church of St. Blasius had
barely escaped. Even pen and ink to sign the
necessary documents of Bach's appointment were
hard to come by. But all was settled, he returned
to Arnstadt, gave in his resignation, and early
in the autumn removed himself and his goods,
in the wagon whose loan he had requested, north-
wards to Mühlhausen. He came there on or
about September 15. The following month he
married his cousin Maria Barbara. For the
ceremony he returned to Arnstadt, and October
17 saw him wending his way to the adjoining
village of Dornheim, where, in the quaint and
simple little church, he and Maria Barbara
exchanged rings and were made man and
wife by Pastor Johann Stauber. With quaintly
solemn words the marriage is recorded in the
register :

"On 17 October 1707 the worthy Johann
Sebastian Bach, bachelor, organist of the
Church of Divi Blasii, Mühlhausen, lawfully
begotten son of the deceased honourable and
distinguished Ambrosius Bach, town's organist
and musician, of Eisenach, to the virtuous
Maria Barbara, spinster, youngest surviving

daughter of the late right worthy and distinguished Michael Bach, organist at Gehren,
here in the house of God, by permission of his
lordship the Count, and after banns duly called
at Arnstadt."[1]

Maria Barbara was born on October 20, 1684,
so she was just five months older than her young
husband—she being within three days of her
twenty-third birthday, which Sebastian did not
reach till the following March. Everything smiled
on them starting out upon their new life together.
The expenses of the move and setting up their
simple home had been assisted by a fortunate
legacy of fifty gulden, which Sebastian's maternal
uncle, Tobias Lämmerhirt, dying at this time,
had left him. Within a week of the wedding
the newly married pair, after paying short visits
to relations, were settled at Mühlhausen. The
place of their dwelling is no longer known—
there was nothing to indicate in 1707 that the
humble abode of a young organist and his bride
would ever be of the least interest to the world.
Owing to the devastations of the fire, they may
have changed their quarters once or twice instead
of going straight into a settled home. But
though we do not know where Bach lived and
worked and watched his wife about her new household affairs, we know, and can still see, the church

[1] *Bach : a Biography*, C. Sanford Terry.

where his duty took him constantly. With its trim towers, its soaring arches, its rich-coloured windows, the Kirche Divi Blasii was a great contrast to the Arnstadt church, and we know enough of Bach's nature to realise how beauty affected him, and especially beauty in connection with the religion which was so deeply rooted in his deep nature. His position and his personal feeling naturally drew his first attention to the organ, and we can think of him testing its powers, by the method which Forkel, on the testimony of Bach's sons, tells us was his way with an organ. He demanded unusual qualities in an organ, for his registration was entirely unconventional, just as his instinctive recognition of the acoustic possibilities of any building was so unerring as to appear uncanny. It is told of him in his later years that he entered the gallery of a large room in the newly built Opera House in Berlin, and at once realised, after glancing at the roof, that a person speaking in a whisper with his face to the wall in one corner would be heard distinctly in the corner diagonally opposite.

Johann Nikolaus Forkel, who was born the year before Bach died, and became his first biographer and the first writer to recognise something of his real stature, had the inestimable advantage of intercourse with Bach's sons, and is therefore one whose opinions and statements are as near the source as we can get. A few quotations from his remarks on "Bach the Organist" will come fittingly here :

"His registration frequently astonished organists and Organ builders, who ridiculed it at first, but were obliged in the end to admit its admirable results and to confess that the Organ gained in richness and sonority.

"Bach's peculiar registration was based on his intimate knowledge of Organ building and of the properties of each individual stop. Very early in his career he made a point of giving to each part of the Organ the utterance best suited to its qualities, and this led him to seek unusual combinations of stops which otherwise would not have occurred to him. Nothing escaped his notice which had the slightest bearing on his art or promised to advance it. . . . Bach's pre-eminent position and his high reputation often caused him to be invited to examine candidates for vacant organistships, and to report on new Organs. In both cases he acted so conscientiously and impartially that he generally made enemies. . . . He could as little prevail on himself to praise a bad instrument as to recommend a bad organist. He was, therefore, severe, though always fair, in the tests he applied, and as he was thoroughly acquainted with the construction of the instrument it was hopeless to attempt to deceive him. First of all he drew out all the stops, to hear the Full Organ. He used to say jokingly that he wanted to find out whether the instrument had good lungs ! Then he gave every part of it a most searching test."[1]

The organ of Divi Blasii at Mühlhausen, which was newly come under Bach's control, did not satisfy his wishes, and the specification still exists in which he set down what he wanted and what the organ needed. It is unnecessary to quote it, as it is purely technical, but we get a little echo of Bach's own voice in the statement that the Gemshorn on the upper manual needed to be replaced by a Viola da Gamba " which will blend admirably " with the Salicional on the Rückpositiv, and his request that the Tremulant be " made to vibrate properly." It is refreshing to know that Bach did not belong to that " superior " class of organist who cannot endure the Tremulant.

One of his first duties at Mühlhausen was to compose music to be performed at a civic function. This cantata, *Gott Ist Mein König*, was performed with much pomp and circumstance at the Marienkirche, whose organist played the continuo, while Sebastian directed the voices and instruments. This cantata, the parts of which were printed at Mühlhausen's expense, was, strange though it seems, the only one of his cantatas that Bach ever saw in print.

While he was at Mühlhausen, Bach not only

[1] Forkel : *Johann Sebastian Bach*, edited by C. Sanford Terry.

wrote music of his own, but collected other music for the church's use—" I have got together from various sources far and near a select collection of sacred *Stücke*," in his own words.

But he was not destined to stay long in Mühlhausen. Difficulties of a religious nature, between the orthodox Lutherans and those who were called Pietists, caused Bach to feel uneasy, and interfered with his wish to serve God by his music. " It has been my constant aim to accord with your desire," he wrote, in his letter of resignation to the Parochial Council, " that church music should be so performed as to exalt God's glory, and, as far as my humble ability has allowed, I have assisted that purpose also in the villages, where the taste for music is growing."

Further on in this letter comes a little personal sidelight : " Moreover," he remarks mildly, " If I may say so respectfully, frugal as is my household, I have not enough to live on."

When he wrote that letter he knew that a few months would see the arrival of his first child, that Catharina Dorothea who was to die, unmarried, twenty-four years after his own decease. All these things combined had induced him to accept the post that had been offered to him at Weimar by the Duke of Sachsen-Weimar. His resignation was received regretfully by the Mühlhausen authorities, with the condition attached that he would continue to supervise the alterations to the organ. Short as had been his dwelling among them, Bach and his wife evidently took with them on their departure many friendly regards, and when, in the following year, the improved organ was completed, he came over from Weimar to display its qualities.

It was during this short sojourn at Mühlhausen that Bach began his life as a " Master " musician. Up to that time he had been learning, experimenting, wandering. Then he became " Master," married—the two were almost inevitably linked together in the domestic German mind—and began, also after the German custom, to take pupils into his house. The first of these pupils was Johann Martin Schubart, who was only five years younger, and was born in the same month as Bach. The deep attachment which his best pupils always felt for him, as exemplified in certain stories which remain, was ideally shown by the first of them. Martin Schubart was for ten years Bach's pupil, companion, and assistant, living under his roof, first at Mühlhausen and then moving with him to Weimar, where, in 1717, he succeeded him, though he only held the post for four years, dying young. In some cases, father and sons were, in succession, pupils of Bach, as with the family of Krebs. One of the sons, Johann Ludwig, was Bach's pupil for nine years, and became an admirable musician, and it is recorded that his master made a little joke on their respective names (which mean brook and crab), and said that he " was the only crab in his brook ! " In a testimonial which he gave the young man, Bach said : " I am persuaded that we have trained him, especially in music, in which he distinguished himself among us by his playing on the clavier, violin, and lute, and equally in composition, in such a way that he should have no hesitation in letting people hear him, as will appear more fully when he does so. I therefore trust that he will obtain Divine assistance to help him to advancement, and I recommend him once again most heartily."

The wording of that testimonial reveals something of Sebastian's nature to us—it was written, of course, in his mature years. We feel his solidity and restraint, his immensely high standard as to what it meant to be a musician, thus making unsuitable any facile enthusiasm. He continued to teach from the Mühlhausen days right to the end of his life, and among the outstanding names of his pupils—apart from his highly gifted sons, Friedemann, Carl Philipp Emanuel, and Johann Christian, known as the " English " Bach—are Agricola, Kirnberger, Goldberg (of the " Goldberg Variations "), Vogler, Müthell, Kittel, his nephew Johann Bernard, and his son-in-law Altnikol. On their own statement many of his pupils confessed that the hours they spent at his feet were among the happiest of their lives.

One young man, Heinrich Nikolaus Gerber,
came to Leipzig, when Bach was Cantor there,
with the express wish of becoming his pupil—
but his reverent awe of Bach was so great that
for a whole year he could not summon up courage
to approach him. At last another musician took
pity on his shyness and took him to the Cantor's
house : " Bach received him, as a native of
Schwarzburg, with particular kindness, and ever
after called him his fellow-countryman. He
promised to give him the instruction he craved,
and at once asked him if he had been diligent in
playing fugues. At the first lesson he set his
Inventions before him ; after he had studied these
to Bach's satisfaction, he gave him a series of
suites, and then the *Temperirte Clavier.* This Bach
played through to him three times with his
inimitable skill, and he accounted those the
happiest hours of his life when Bach, under
pretence of not being in the humour to teach,
would sit down to his excellent instrument, and
the hours seemed to be but minutes."

Johann Caspar Vogler became, as Bach himself
declared, one of his best organ pupils. Another
pupil, Johann Philip Kirnberger, probably from
jealousy for his master's eminence, was very
wroth when he heard that some critic had dared
to put Vogler on a level with Bach himself. He
broke out into protest : " If we ask, ' Who is
Vogler ? ' after much enquiry we discover that

he is a *bürgermeister* and organist of Weimar, and a pupil of Bach, but not the most eminent by a long way ! "

But not a few of these young men, so long dead, held while living that their best claim to remembrance would be that they had been " pupils of Bach." And to the best of their ability they handed on the gift they had received. Had it not been for their faithful copying, we should have lost some of the compositions of Bach's we now possess. The only manuscript of one of the organ Preludes and Fugues is in a copy made by a pupil of Kittel. The great C minor Organ Fantasia would be lost were it not for a copy made by Krebs a few months after Bach's death. Moreover, they handed down by their writings and teachings certain traditions of Bach's methods and aphorisms to a generation which held them but slackly, but did not quite let them fall into the dust of oblivion. When the Bach revival came, these traditions were to be gathered up and cherished. But that is matter for a later chapter.

CHAPTER III

So, with the first of these pupils, Martin Schubart,
young Sebastian Bach and his wife moved in
1708 to Weimar, to the quiet and serious Court
of Duke Wilhelm Ernst. The Duke, a middle-
aged man, separated from his wife after a short
and unhappy marriage, was engrossed in religion,
education, and grave consideration of the arts.
So little did he countenance frivolity that he and
his Court retired at nine of the clock in summer
and eight in winter, and all was still and silent
in the Castle after those early hours. But this
gravity of life would not appear depressing to
Bach, who himself was of an earnest disposition,
and who had at his domestic hearth what the
Duke lacked in his Castle, the company of a
wife he loved and the expectation of a child.
The Duke's interest in church music agreed with
Bach's own strong inclination—the word dedication seems almost more fitting—in that direction,
and the post of organist to the Castle Chapel
suited him in every way. What is called the
" Weimar period " in Bach's life was to prove

gloriously fruitful, as a remembrance of the works belonging to this time will show—" the consummate compositions of the Weimar period," as Dr. Albert Schweitzer calls them. The Castle Chapel had received the name of " Weg zur Himmelsburg "—the Way to the Heavenly City —and we may imagine that in a special sense it deserved that name when Bach, in the dawning glory of his powers, played upon that organ the music he had himself composed. It was not a powerful organ, but had two manuals and a good full-toned pedal. It served to inspire Bach to create such organ music as had not existed in the world up to that time. Bach holds the place of the greatest organ composer and organ player in the history of music, so it is somewhat strange to realise that it was only in the early part of his life that he was officially an organist—the posts at Arnstadt and at Mühlhausen, held for so short a time, and the years from 1708 to 1717 when he was at Weimar. When he left Weimar in 1717, to the year of his death in 1750, he was never any more officially an organist, though at Leipzig he had organs at his disposal. So the flower of his life in connection with the instrument which there can be no doubt was above all others beloved by him, was compressed into little more than a decade. If all the wealth of Bach's choral and instrumental music were lost—if the Passions, the great B minor Mass, the marvellous

Church Cantatas, the Brandenburg Concertos, the
" Well-tempered Clavier " disappeared from all
knowledge—and only the organ music remained,
we still should feel that Bach was one of the
greatest composers who ever visited this earth.
And this in spite of the fact that the bulk of his
organ compositions is very small compared with
the rest of his works—only four volumes and a
portion of a fifth compared with fifty-seven in
the great Bachgesellschaft edition.

In the most valuable, though still incomplete,
edition of Bach's organ works, edited by Widor
and Schweitzer, the editors say : " The compositions from the late Weimar period form a class
by themselves. The Preludes develop only a
single thought. The fugue-themes are simple,
concise, unornamented, almost austere, they
discover scarcely any of the animated running
figurations found in the works of the first Master-
Period."

To this period at Weimar we owe such brilliant
things as the Prelude and Fugue in D major,
the Toccata and Fugue in D minor, whose dazzling
effect when played by Bach himself may be
imagined, the lovely tender " Little E minor "
Prelude and Fugue, the delicate solemnity of the
Canzona in D minor, the majesty of the Passacaglia. At the close of the Weimar period comes
that particular treasure of the Bach organist,
the *Orgelbüchlein*, which in the enduring loveliness

of its contents goes so far beyond the humble title
that Bach himself gave it : " A Little Book for the
Organ, wherein the Beginner may learn to
perform Chorals of every Kind and also acquire
skill in the Use of the Pedal, which is treated
uniformly obbligato throughout. To God alone
the praise be given For what's herein to man's
use written."

The most gifted of organists for over two centuries have not succeeded in drawing all the sweetness out of the honeycomb of the *Orgelbüchlein*
which Bach so modestly offered to the " Beginning Organist." What riches of new beauty the
young Sebastian brought with him and developed
in the organ-loft at Weimar.

When he arrived in Weimar, he would find
with pleasure that a connection of his own was
organist at the church of St. Peter and St. Paul.
This was Johann Gottfried Walther, who is now
best remembered for the *Musical Lexicon* he
compiled and published at Leipzig in 1732,
while Bach was still alive. The two musicians
became very friendly—Bach was godfather to
Walther's eldest son ; they amused themselves
by exchanging specimens of their musical skill
in four-part canons. Another of the few personal
anecdotes we have concerning Bach shows him
in relation to Walther. Sebastian had apparently
made in his friend's presence the not very extravagant statement, considering his powers, that he

believed he could play any composition unhesitatingly at sight. Whereupon Walther decided
to trip him up. " Having invited Bach to breakfast one morning "—to continue the story in
Forkel's words, as translated by Dr. Sanford
Terry—" he placed on the clavier, among other
music, a piece which, at first glance, seemed per-
fectly easy. On his arrival, Bach, as was his
custom, sat down at the clavier to play or look
through the music. Meanwhile his friend was in
the next room preparing breakfast. In a short
time, Bach took up the piece of music destined
to change his opinion and began to play it. He
had not proceeded far before he came to a passage
at which he stopped. After a look at it he began
again, only to stop at the same place. ' No,'
he called out to his friend, who was laughing
heartily in the next room, ' the man does not
exist who can play everything at sight. It can't
be done.' With that he got up from the clavier
in some annoyance."

Bach's first Christmas at Weimar was happily
marked by the birth of his first child, a daughter,
Catharina Dorothea. All his children by his
first wife, with the exception of the last son,
Leopold Augustus, were born at Weimar. They
were Catharina Dorothea, born in 1708, Wilhelm
Friedemann, that most gifted of his sons, born in
1710 ; twins, a boy and a girl, born and died in
1713 ; Carl Philipp Emanuel, born in 1714 ; and

Johann Gottfried Bernhard, born in 1715. The daughter and the two eldest sons, both of whom became distinguished musicians, outlived their father ; the two younger sons died before him. His first wife, Maria Barbara, has retired into a complete and modest obscurity from which no portrait, no anecdote, rescues her. We hear her singing for a moment in the organ-loft at Arnstadt, we have the register of her marriage, the dates of the births of her seven children, and then, with a complete suddenness and self-obliteration, she dies. But it was not at Weimar she died. It is reasonable to assume her musical, and therefore sympathetic to her husband, both from her heritage as a Bach by birth, and from the record of her singing. That is all we know of her.

Of Bach's friends at Weimar we know a little more. During his time there Christoph Kiese-wetter, his former master in his boyhood at Ohrdruf, came as Rector to the Weimar Gymnasium. Three years later Johann Matthias Gesner was appointed Conrector, and was a man with a true and understanding love of music, with whom Bach began a friendship which was to be renewed and deepened in years to come at Leipzig. The Custodian of the ducal library was Salomo Franck, the hymn-writer, with whose deep religious feeling Bach found himself in natural sympathy. Franck had written two volumes of

DB

cantata texts, and when Bach was appointed
Concertmeister to the Duke in 1714, he used
Salomo's libretti exclusively for his Weimar
cantatas, with one exception. Another poet,
Christoph Lorber, also belonged to the Duke's
cultured Court, and as he also cared much for
music, he would not fail to seek the friendship of
the young organist, in spite of the considerable
difference in their ages. The cantor of the
gymnasium, Georg Theodor Reineccius, was a
sound musician, and as Bach asked him to be
godfather to the small daughter who was born
and died in 1713, it is plain that their association
was more than a formal one. So we can imagine
the young Bach—he was twenty-three when he
went to Weimar, and thirty-two when he left
it—in surroundings that were quiet and cultivated,
in a settled home of his own, with his young
family beginning to grow round him, earning a
salary that, in spite of his increasing expenses,
did not force him to the Mühlhausen statement
that he " could with difficulty live." It was a
period of his life full of fruit, and full of content.
From Weimar his reputation was beginning
to spread to surrounding towns and villages,
though Mattheson's statement in 1716 can
hardly be accused of too extravagant enthusiasm when he wrote, " I have seen things by
the famous organist Herr Johann Sebastian
Bach, of Weimar, which, both for Church use

and for keyed instruments, are certainly so conceived that we cannot but highly esteem the man."

Bach was in demand increasingly as the rumour of his wonderful powers spread among his country-men, to test new organs and new organists, and to give himself what we should now call "re-citals." There are testimonies from his pupils as to the wonder of his organ improvisations— "his admirable and learned manner of fanciful playing," to the "novelty, singularity, expressive-ness and beauty of his inspirations at the moment, and their perfect rendering." Kirnberger has given a careful account of the intricate and mar-vellous music that flowed from his fingers "when he sat down to the organ, irrespective of Divine service, as he was often requested to do by strangers." It is pleasant to recall that on one occasion when he had been praised for his superb playing, Bach remarked calmly, "There is nothing very wonderful about it ; you have only to hit the right notes at the right moment, and the instrument does the rest."

In 1713 the Liebfrauenkirche at Halle, the town where Handel was born, and whose master Zachau had been organist of that church, was in need of an organist for its very fine newly built organ of sixty-three speaking stops. Bach visited Halle and played upon this organ, and thereby so impressed the worthy citizens that they sent

after him to Weimar a " Vocation," and expressed
their desire that he should take up his abode
among them. The negotiations over this matter
are somewhat complicated, and the letters from
Halle to the " right worthy and competent Herr
Johann Sebastian Bach," and from Bach to Halle,
too long to quote. Bach was evidently tempted
by this offer, not by the salary, but by the organ,
which was much finer than his organ at Weimar.
But he was in the employ of a prince who did not
easily grant permission to remove from his service,
and the conditions of the Halle post required
modification before they would suit Bach's needs,
which modifications the Halle authorities were
disinclined to allow. Bach had his wife and
growing family to consider, he could not rashly
let go of one post before he was certain of the
other—so he temporised. The fact that about
this time the Duke made Bach his *Concertmeister*
and increased his stipend, caused the gibe to be
current in Halle that Bach had unworthily used
the Halle offer to better his position—a suggestion
which it is unnecessary to refute. Bach had acted,
as he always did, with caution, and due regard
for the necessities of his family. Rashness was
not one of his characteristics, neither was in-
temperance nor any form of self-indulgence. That
he was at times inclined to be irritable, that he
was capable of pugnacity and obstinacy in defence
of his just rights, we know. But essentially Bach

was " Well-tempered "—adjusted, as it were, to all the keys of life.

His new position in the ducal Court as *Concert-meister* gave him further opportunities, and led his eager mind to the study of chamber music and the consideration of Italian forms of the art which had hitherto not come much in his way. Italian violin concertos attracted him considerably, and he arranged sixteen of Vivaldi's concertos for the clavier and three for the organ. It may safely be assumed that he played them himself on the instrument for which they were originally written, as he was accomplished both on the violin and the viola. It is said that in a string quartet he preferred to play the viola, for so he felt himself " in the middle of the harmony." He did not neglect Italian organ music ; and the great Frescobaldi, that sixteenth-century organist who had said so haughtily, " Whoever can understand me, let him do so," certainly found in Bach one who could completely understand him. A copy of Frescobaldi's *Fiori Musicali*, one hundred and four pages entirely written out in Bach's own hand, is in existence, dated 1714. " Indeed," as Dr. Sanford Terry says in *Bach : the Historical Approach*, " there is little music from Palestrina onwards of which there are not copies in his industrious script." Bach's Canzona for the organ bears traces of the Frescobaldi influence. He also wrote an organ fugue on a theme of

Legrenzi's, and used themes by Corelli and Albinoni. He transmuted, in his own marvellous way, all the knowledge and experience that came to him into music.

Towards the end of 1714, Bach visited Cassel, and created astonishment and admiration by the brilliance and technical mastery of his organ playing. He played at the Hofkirche before the German Prince who later became King of Sweden, and Constantin Bellermann has left on record an impression of the occasion: " His feet, flying over the pedals as though they were winged, made the notes reverberate like thunder in a storm." The Prince pulled a costly ring from his finger and gave it to the organist. " Now bethink you," Bellermann goes on, " if Bach's skilful feet deserved such a bounty, what gift must the Prince have offered to reward his hands as well ? "

Evidently the Prince thought Bach's hands were beyond the resources of his treasury, for he made no further offering. Indeed, in the whole of his life, Bach's rewards from such sources were but meagre, and the honours bestowed upon him were of the scantiest description, despite his connection with various Courts. Count von Kayserling, for whom he wrote the " Goldberg Variations," bestowed a snuff-box upon him containing a hundred louis d'or. He was given the official title of Court Composer to the Court of Dresden—after he had several times asked for

it. Frederick the Great invited him to Potsdam
in his last years, and as he performed on one of
the new Silbermann fortepianos of which the
King had a considerable collection, the story is
that he stood behind " Old Bach " exclaiming
delightedly, " There is only one Bach ! " Certainly the King of Prussia never said a truer thing.

At Weimar, Bach began composing the Church
Cantatas with which his name is so essentially
associated. He had written one or two earlier
ones than those of the Weimar period, but it was
there that he first seriously set his foot on the path
he was to follow—with a brief slackening in out-
put at Cöthen—with such amazing industry, with
such unflagging genius, for the rest of his life.
At Weimar he first found, in the works of Neumeister and Salomo Franck, Cantata texts that
appealed to his sensitive and mystical imagination. He was curiously, at times almost childishly,
responsive to the meaning and the associations
of words. Their pictorial quality produced a
definite response in him. One of his Weimar
pupils, Gotthilf Ziegler, who became organist at
Halle, writing in 1746, said : " Herr Capellmeister
Bach, who is still living, instructed me when
playing hymns not to treat the melody as if it
alone were important, but to interpret the words
through the melody." Bach's mind had definite
musical reactions to particular words and verbal
images. Much research has been given to this

fascinating subject by Spitta and Schweitzer and others. It is impossible to enter upon it here, but some idea of what may be called Bach's musical idiom when dealing with words is essential to a proper understanding of the cantatas and necessary to a full appreciation of the *Orgel-büchlein*. Indeed, one of the mysteries of Bach is that it seems impossible in one human lifetime to do more than just begin to understand him. Yet he created all this body of music, which has engaged the deepest researches of musicians and scholars for generations, while he was fully occupied in living an industrious, hard-working, everyday kind of life. That the creative genius is a thing entirely apart from circumstance, and even from character, is a fact that cannot be denied, as it is proved by so many strange instances.

The sacred cantatas immensely outnumber the secular ones, as was natural from the nature of Bach's employment during the latter half of his life. The earliest of these secular cantatas, *Was mir behagt*, was composed by Bach and produced at Weissenfels on the occasion of a festive visit of his Duke Wilhelm Ernst to Duke Christian of Sachsen-Weissenfels. How amazed these ducal personages would have been could they have guessed that the only interest posterity was likely to take in their pompous entertainments would be due to the presence there of an obscure *Concertmeister*.

Soon after this visit in the train of his Duke, Bach was invited to Halle to examine and report on the then completed organ of the Liebfrauen-kirche. From the letter of acceptance he sent, it is plain that this invitation gratified him and marked the end of any coolness in his relations with the authorities of that town. When he arrived in Halle on April 28, 1716, and met the colleagues, Christian Friedrich Rolle and Johann Kuhnan, who were jointly to report with him on the organ, he found generous arrangements made for their comfort and entertainment. They stayed in Halle till May 3, and servants and coach-men were specially set apart to wait upon them. Two days were devoted to examining the organ, and two more to writing and delivering their report, which was very favourable. On the Sunday the new organ was formally opened and dedicated, and after that ceremony there was a lavish banquet. The menu survives, and raises a certain astonishment with its mixture of viands —beef and pike and smoked ham, sausages, spinach, peas, boiled pumpkin, mutton, candied lemon-peel, cherries, radishes, roast veal, lettuce, asparagus salad. No doubt musicians who had worked so hard and—can we doubt it in Bach's case ?—played so magnificently on the new organ, needed all this " fine confused feeding."

On the last Sunday of the same month, which was Whit-Sunday, Bach produced in the Duke's

Chapel his first cantata written to Neumeister's words, *Wer mich liebet*.

The invitation to Halle and his distinguished treatment while there showed how Sebastian's fame was spreading, and the same year gives us another instance of this recognition and another of the valuable little personal glimpses of him. A certain French musician of considerable fame, Jean Louis Marchand, was travelling in Germany at this time, as he had fallen out of favour at the Court of Versailles. He was full of conceit in his own musical powers and made no secret of it. Bach was begged to meet the self-confident Frenchman and support the dignity of German music—" Though little enough they think of German musicians," he once said with unusual bitterness, " but leave them to shift for themselves, so that many are too overwhelmed with cares for their daily bread to be able to perfect, far less to distinguish, themselves."

This sort of contest had small appeal to Bach. But, being in Dresden at the time, he was induced to suggest a meeting to Marchand, at which each of them should agree to any musical test proposed by the other. Marchand accepted, and the contest was arranged to take place at a Court official's house, before a learned and fashionable audience. Bach arrived punctually—one has the feeling that Bach believed in punctuality—but Marchand was not there. After waiting some time, a messenger was sent to his lodging to tell him that the company awaited his appearance. But it was then discovered that the Frenchman, having secretly taken an opportunity to hear Bach play, had acknowledged the quality of his opponent by departing that morning from Dresden by express coach. So Bach had the field to himself, and played to the delight and admiration of his listeners. We do not know what he played on this occasion, but it was told of him in later years that whenever he sat down to the keyboard he always preferred to begin by playing the music of some other composer before he let his own mind have free play in improvisation. We know that he was too good a musician to disparage Marchand's abilities. Bach's fellow Thuringian and contemporary, Jakob Adlung, himself an organist and the author of important works on music, said of Marchand's compositions for the clavier : " They never really pleased me but once, namely, when I spoke to the Capellmeister Bach of his challenge when he was staying here "—Adlung was writing at Erfurt—" and told him I had these suites by me ; and he played them to me in his manner, that is to say, very smoothly and artistically."

Bach's life offers us several little glimpses like that of his playing or explaining the music of other composers in order to draw attention to its merits. As he was always not only willing, but eager, to learn from other musicians, so he never showed any signs of jealousy towards others' merits, though he was not lacking in a proper sense of his own worth.

Soon after this affair with Marchand, which considerably increased his fame, he suffered a curious eclipse at Weimar. The old Court Capellmeister Drese had long been past his work, much of which had been done by Bach himself. When at last the old man died, it was not unnatural that Bach should expect to receive the post. The Duke passed him over and gave it to a far less competent and suitable person, Drese's son, and Bach felt, with justice, that he had been unfairly passed over. Other matters were rendering his position at Weimar difficult. The Duke was of a severe disposition, with strong feudal views towards his dependants. He was on very bad terms with his nephew, Duke Ernst August, and forbade any members of his Court and *Capelle* to have intercourse with him. Bach, who found the young Duke musical and sympathetic, had got involved in these prohibitions. It is a long and tiresome story, of which this is the barest outline. But owing to his relations with the young Duke, who at this time married the sister of Prince Leopold of Anhalt-Cöthen, Bach was introduced to the notice of his next patron. Prince Leopold was very musical—" *ein grosser Kenner und Liebhaber der Musik* "—and so soon as he was brought in contact with Bach, recognised his quality and desired that he should become his *Capellmeister*. So Bach requested his release from Weimar. We do not know the details of what happened, whether he made some angry remarks, as well as being urgent " in obstinately demanding his instant dimission." All we know is the extra-ordinary result. The Duke forcibly detained him —actually put him under arrest in the justice-room—from November 6 to December 2, 1717, when, as the ducal secretary states, he was released " with a grudging permission to retire from the Duke's service."[1]

It was a curious ending to Bach's years at Weimar. But, knowing his disposition, it is certain that a month's forced abstention from active duties was not wasted by him, and it is thought that he employed this time in planning the *Orgelbüchlein* and partly writing it. Rarely has so lovely a fruit come from imprisonment. As Spitta says, " the narrower the circle in which Bach had to turn, the deeper he went." This remark was made about the " Little Book for the Organ," though not applied to his detention. This period of " exceptional leisure," as Dr. Sanford Terry calls the month of Bach's imprison-ment, was used in the production of the *Orgel-büchlein*, which contains ninety-two sheets, and is bound in paper boards with leather back and corners. The copy in Bach's own hand is the

[1] *Bach : a Biography*, C. Sanford Terry.

only complete one in existence, though on these pages a much larger work was planned than was actually achieved. Bach intended to write one hundred and sixty-four Choral Preludes for the organ ; he only completed forty-six, and the blank pages contain simply the names of the melodies he had proposed to adorn. It is almost possible to regret that the Duke had not kept him longer in a durance that he turned to such beneficent use. But the *Orgelbüchlein* was Bach's swan-song as an organist—never, after Weimar, was he to hold an official post as organist again. *Capellmeister* and composer of chamber music, Cantor and composer of sacred cantatas, were the paths he was henceforth to tread. We must admire the simplicity of Bach's greatness, which accepted the conditions imposed upon him by the necessities of earning his bread, and with no thought of hardship or turmoil of temperament, produced his music—apparently with as little consciousness of its greatness as had the most reluctant small Thomaner boy who, in the Leipzig years, was obliged to sing it.

By Christmas, 1717, Bach and his family were settled at Cöthen—his first pupil, Martin Schubart, taking his master's place as organist at the Schloss Chapel in Weimar.

Bach's new patron, Prince Leopold of Anhalt-Cöthen, was some nine years younger than his *Capellmeister*—a romantic and musical young

Prince, who had performed the "grand tour" of Europe, including a visit to England, and who played the violin, *viol da gamba*, and clavier, and, in Bach's own words, "loved and understood music." This was a recommendation that could not always be given to princes, and Bach apparently hoped that he might end his days in Cöthen, in surroundings which—apart from the lack of the organ and the religious usage he was accustomed to, the Court at Cöthen being "reformed" into a bleak severity—were almost ideal. Cöthen offered him a young and enthusiastic prince, who, though of the "Reformed" Faith, had no bigotry and believed that his subjects should be "protected in their freedom of conscience." At Cöthen, Bach had a good salary and position, and a *Capelle* unusually well equipped with excellent instruments, for which he was to write the enchanting "Brandenburg" music. When he was at Leipzig, Bach must have looked back with considerable regret upon the equipment of the Cöthen orchestra, as he contemplated the battered instruments belonging to the Thomasschule.

Dr. Sanford Terry has come to the conclusion that the Bach family probably had their quarters in the Castle itself, and he says it is "agreeable to associate him with a fabric that preserves the features with which he was familiar, to picture him making music with his *Collegium Musicum* in its candle-lit apartments, or taking his walks abroad across the bridged moat between the sentries into the exercise ground, where sleek horses stood in comfortable stables, and the princely carriages were visible within the great doors. A happy playground for the young Bachs this sometime tilting-ground must have been."

The last of the children born to Anna Maria and Sebastian Bach, Leopold Augustus, was baptised in the Castle Chapel in November 1718, the Duke standing as godfather and bestowing his name.

Bach had hardly settled in Cöthen before he was invited to visit Leipzig to examine and report on the new organ in the Paulinerkirche. He had no colleagues in this examination, which was entrusted to him alone. His detailed and careful report survives. On this occasion he also conducted a performance of his Advent cantata, *Nun Komm, der Heiden Heiland*, at one of the Leipzig churches, and on the manuscript of this cantata there are notes in his sensitive handwriting as to the order of the morning service, showing that he took care to inform himself exactly as to an unfamiliar ritual.

His years at Cöthen proceeded pleasantly. The somewhat secluded life of the Castle was varied by visits with the young Duke, who, as Spitta says, " soon became aware of the treasure he had found in Bach, and showed it in the frankest manner. He could not bear to part with him—he took him on his travels, and loved him as a friend ; and after his early death Bach always cherished his memory." Bach returned the kindness of his patron by writing a serenade for the Prince's birthday, the words of which, as well as the music, are generally believed to be Bach's own production. There is a simple sincerity about them which does not suggest the work of some merely official writer. On another and later occasion Bach is known to have written a little poem to a new-born princeling, which he presented with the first Partita of the *Clavierübung*. It is a rather quaint and tender little poem, and begins :

Most Serene, Sweet Prince, wrapped in thy swaddling
 clothes,
Although thy princely look betokens riper years,
Forgive me if I should awaken thee from sleep
By allowing my page of melody to pay thee its respects.
It is the first-fruit brought by my lyre,
Thou art the first Princeling to be embraced by thy mother,
She should sing it first in thy honour,
For thou, like this page, art a first-born in the world.

And it ends :

So, Prince, full of hope, I will play to thee again
When thy fulfilment is more than a thousandfold.
I only desire always, as now, to feel the inspiration,
That I may be, Serene Prince,
  Thy most earnest servant,
                          Bach.

During his years at Cöthen, Bach was industriously engaged in composing music, and the Court
bookbinder industriously engaged in binding it for
the ducal library.   Among his compositions of
this period are the six Brandenburg Concertos
—" his earliest essays in absolute instrumental
music on the grand scale.   They are a remarkable
expression of his fertile and adventurous mind."[1]
How fresh and enchanting they are, all who have
heard them know.   They were dedicated to a
fortunate—and thenceforth immortal—Markgraf
of Brandenburg in 1721.   Bach also wrote at
Cöthen brilliant things for the keyboard, which he
undoubtedly performed himself, such as the
radiant Chromatic Fantasia and Fugue, the Fantasia and Fugue in A minor, and the Toccatas in
C minor and F sharp minor.   To these things, as
to so much of Bach's work, may be applied the
words of one who nearly a hundred years after
Bach's death was Cantor of the Leipzig Thomasschule : " The spirit of youth in Music is like a
drop of dew in amber, no time can harden it."
It was at Cöthen also that Bach produced the first
half of his " Well-tempered Clavier "—the second
half was not written till twenty-two years later—
which Spitta says " reflects the whole of the
Cöthen period of Bach's life with its peace and
contemplation, its deep and solemn self-collected-
ness."   Did Bach realise what a marvellous gift

[1] *The Music of Bach*, C. Sanford Terry.

he was bestowing on the world in this work?
We cannot know. We only know that in the
autograph title-page he says modestly that he
"composed and put forth" the twenty-four
Preludes and Fugues "For the Use and Profit of
young Musicians anxious to learn, and as a
Pastime for others already expert in the Art."

The inexhaustible fountain of his genius was
flowing freely. He wrote so much music that few
musicians, though they give a lifetime to it, can
claim a complete knowledge of his works, and
there is nothing he wrote, not even the simplest
Two-Part Invention, that has not some touch of
the inexhaustible about it—a quality of perpetual
freshness, like running water. As simple, as
commonplace, as running water—and as much a
miracle.

But the "Well-tempered Clavier" was still to
be written when the summer of 1720 brought a
heavy loss to Bach. He had accompanied Prince
Leopold on one of his frequent visits to Carlsbad,
leaving his wife, as he thought, for a short time.
When he returned to his home at Cöthen it was to
receive the news that she was dead and laid in her
grave. What illness killed her, with apparently
so little warning, we do not know. Bach has left
no written record of his shock and grief. He was
thirty-five years old, he had four surviving
children, the eldest a girl of twelve. Three
children had died—in those days that was

regarded as almost inevitable. But the death of his wife, the girl who was his first love, who had sung so happily in his organ-loft at Arnstadt, was a much deeper loss. By tradition and upbringing the Bachs were a home-loving race.

CHAPTER IV

MARIA BARBARA BACH had died early in July 1720. On December 3, 1721, Sebastian married Anna Magdalena Wilcken, or Wülckens, at his own lodging at the Castle, by special permission of Prince Leopold. Of Anna Magdalena, as of Maria Barbara, no known portrait survives, though one in oils by Cristofori is known to have been painted of her, but unfortunately it has disappeared. Nevertheless, through many little touches and incidents, Anna Magdalena leaves a definite impression of sweetness and simplicity and devotion to her great husband. In a music-book Sebastian made for her, there are some wedding verses he wrote, which may be taken as her picture :

> *Your servant, sweetest maiden Bride :*
> *Joy be with you this morning !*
> *To see you in your flowery crown*
> *And wedding-day adorning*
> *Would fill with joy the sternest soul.*

> *What wonder, as I meet you,*
> *That my fond heart and loving lips*
> *O'erflow with song to greet you ?*

She was only just over twenty when she came to
meet her bridegroom, and Bach himself was
nearly thirty-seven—a considerable difference in
their ages, but it caused no rift in their happiness.
Her youth made her the more naturally her
husband's pupil, which she evidently and eagerly
became, being gifted with a beautiful soprano
voice, and coming of a musical stock. Her
maternal grandfather was an organist, her father
was Court Trumpeter at Weissenfels. She herself
was a Court singer, and her earnings helped the
Bach household. Her husband made a *Clavier-
Büchlein vor Anna Magdalena Bachin* the year after
their marriage, and in 1725 a larger book, with
her initials stamped in gold on the green cover,
which is a sort of musical miscellany, containing
music of all kinds written out by them both, while
in Bach's own hand are the rules for playing from
a figured bass, with a note at the end which says
that the sequel must be taught by word of mouth.
These two books " display very touchingly,"
Spitta says, " their intimate and tender relations."
Throughout the years of her marriage, Anna
Magdalena assisted her husband in his endless task
of music-copying. She copied out his cantatas,
she copied for him the music of other composers

which he desired to possess—she took up the pen
when his hand flagged or his time was otherwise occupied. She came to write a very good
music-hand, so closely modelled on his that it
sometimes puzzles the experts to distinguish it
from Bach's. All this implies that her yielding
feminine personality took its impress from the
strong nature she lived with for so many years.
The number of her children was many—thirteen
in all, born between the years 1723 and 1742.
The first child was a daughter, who died three
years later, and was followed, at intervals, by six
other daughters, of whom only three lived to
grow up. Of six sons, only three survived infancy,
and the eldest surviving son, Gottfried Heinrich,
was in some way mentally arrested. In the
Family Tree Bach himself made, he wrote of
Gottfried, "He also shows an inclination to
music, especially "—there his handwriting stops
and the sentence is completed by Carl Philipp
Emanuel, "especially as a clavier player. He
was a real genius, but never developed." The
two other sons who attained manhood were
Johann Christoph, whose son Wilhelm Friedrich
was the only direct descendant of Sebastian
present at the unveiling of the Leipzig statue in
1843. The other son, Johann Christian, came to
England and was music-master to Queen Caroline. He died, without issue, in 1782. The
children of Sebastian's first wife who made their

mark in music were Wilhelm Friedemann and
Carl Philipp Emanuel. Something will be said of
them later. Emanuel had a son who bore his
grandfather's name, Johann Sebastian, but turned
his talents to painting instead of music, and died in
Rome at the age of twenty-six. Such, in brief, is
the rather tragic tale of Bach's twenty children—
many deaths among them, few marriages, and, of
those marriages, the offspring undistinguished.
The conclusion is inevitable that the great clan of
the Thuringian Bachs, which for generations had
been climbing steadily to the culmination which
was Johann Sebastian, declined into obscurity
with a sad suddenness. The flower had been
produced, the stock was exhausted.

But all these things were in the far future when
Johann Sebastian married Anna Magdalena.
Their simple wedding was followed, only a week
later, by a very important one. The young
Prince Leopold of Anhalt-Cöthen himself led
a bride to the altar, his cousin Friederica Henrietta of Anhalt-Berneburg—a lady whose portrait
shows a neat little self-satisfied face, with marked
eyebrows and pursed mouth, in richly jewelled
brocaded attire. Five weeks of festivities celebrated the princely nuptials, and music was
performed by the *Capelle*, Bach providing an Ode
which has vanished, like many other of his compositions. No doubt he and his young wife enjoyed
a discreet share in all the gaieties. But, as it

proved, the new Princess was to be the cause of
Bach leaving Cöthen for Leipzig, where he was
destined to spend the rest of his life.

Even before his Prince's marriage he had been
thinking of the possibility of a change. His work as
Capellmeister at Cöthen had really diverted his
career from the path he had definitely intended to
follow, the dedication of his music to the service
of the Church. At Cöthen there was no scope
for all the stores of religious music shut up within
his breast. The organ there was too small to
tempt him to produce and perform such organ
works as were the fruit of his " Weimar period."
It is evident that he felt the organ calling him.
Soon after his first wife's death, he had paid
another visit to Hamburg, and played on the fine
four-manual organ of the Catharinenkirche,
where the aged and famous Adam Reinken was
still organist, as he had been in Bach's youth.
Reinken was old, his long day was drawing to its
close, many must have been the thoughts and
memories in his mind as he listened to Bach, who
played for more than two hours, and for nearly
half an hour improvised magnificently on the
chorale *An Wasserflüssen Babylon*. At its conclusion,
he came up to Bach and said, with all the solemnity of his years and position, " I thought this art
was dead, but I perceive that it still lives in you."
Bach would be deeply moved by this tribute from
the old organist whom many years before, in his

eager youth, he had walked many miles to hear. There was in Hamburg another fine organ of four manuals—at the Jakobikirche, and, as the organist had died a month or two before Bach's visit, the post was vacant. Bach offered himself for this post—possibly the shock of his wife's recent death had unsettled his mind and made him feel that a change of scene would be welcome. There were seven other candidates, but, as the examination was to be held at a time when Bach was obliged to return to his Prince at Cöthen, he was told that it would not be necessary for him to submit to the formal tests. After his playing in the Catherinenkirche, and Reinken's words, that was no great concession. Bach, apparently, had promised to write from Cöthen saying definitely whether he was willing to take the post, if chosen, but, as the letter has perished, the form of his answer remains uncertain. What is certain is that an organist of complete obscurity was elected, for he had paid over the sum of four thousand marks into the treasury of the church.

Erdmann Neumeister was the chief preacher at the Jakobikirche, and he was so indignant over this business that he would not speak to the new organist. At Christmas-time of that year, he " expounded very beautifully," as his contemporary Mattheson wrote, " the gospel concerning the angelic music at the birth of Christ, which, very naturally, gave him the opportunity of expressing his opinions as to the recent event as regarded the rejected artist, and of ending his discourse with this noteworthy *epiphonema*. He believed quite certainly that if one of the angels of Bethlehem came from Heaven, who played divinely, and desired to be organist to the Jakobikirche, if he had no money he would have nothing to do but to fly away again."

Thus Sebastian Bach had to yield to one who, in Mattheson's phrase, " could prelude with thalers better than he could with his fingers."

It was not to Hamburg that Bach was to go, nor in Cöthen that he was to stay. Since his Prince's marriage, the Court at Cöthen was slowly changing its ways. In a long personal letter written from Leipzig—like all Bach's letters it is curiously trimmed with foreign words, he used Latin, French, Italian, even English words in this way—he told his old friend Georg Erdmann of his circumstances : " My *Serenissimus* married a Bernburg wife, and in consequence, so it seemed, his musical *inclination* abated, while his new Princess proved to be an *amusa*." Possibly, too, the new Princess was a little jealous of her husband's attachment to his serious-minded *Capellmeister*, as well as bored by music beyond the scope of her mind. Up to the time of the Duke's marriage, Bach's position at Cöthen had been a pleasant one. Spitta says : " The eager and intelligent interest the Prince took in his art had enabled him entirely to forget how narrow was the musical circle within which he moved there, its exclusive limitation to chamber music, and the absence of all development in the direction of sacred composition. Since, however, it was for this that Bach must have felt himself especially fitted, nothing was needed but some external impulse to make him aware that his genius would not permit him to set up his tent for the rest of his life in this spot, however delightful he might feel it."

Thus circumstances so combined that when the call came to Leipzig, a year and a half after he had married Anna Magdalena, Bach was ready to respond. The move to Leipzig was to be his last—there he was to stay for the rest of his life, and there he was to write the amazing number of his church cantatas, his Passion music, his Mass in B minor, and the second part of his *Wohltemperirte Clavier*. Of the last work—in scale the smallest of the compositions mentioned—Dr. Schweitzer says : " Whoever has once felt this wonderful tranquillity has comprehended the mysterious spirit that has here expressed all it knew and felt of life in the secret language of tone, and will render Bach the thanks we render only to the great souls to whom it is given to reconcile men with life and bring them peace."

In a rough classification, Weimar had produced his organ music ; Cöthen his chamber music ;

while from Leipzig was to come the immortal voice of his sacred music. An earlier century than his would surely have painted angels clustered on the steep roof of the Thomasschule where that music was written and the steeper roof of the Thomaskirche where it was first performed.

The post of Cantor of the Thomasschule in Leipzig had fallen vacant through the death of Johann Kuhnan in the summer of 1722. There were several quite important candidates for the position, among whom Bach did not at first appear. Two of these candidates, Telemann and Graupner, were elected in succession, and, for reasons which it is not necessary to detail, failed to take up the post bestowed upon them. Then Bach expressed his willingness to become a candidate, and, after a little delay, the cantorship became his in May 1723. The authorities of the Thomasschule could have been in no doubt as to the quality of the man they were getting, though it is recorded that a member of the Council made the strange statement that as the best musicians (the two first elected candidates) were not available, " *müsse man mittlere nehmen* "—in other words take what one can get ! So Leipzig got Bach, while the poor councillor was left looking sadly after the retreating figures of the " best musicians."

Bach himself felt it was a step down to become Cantor after having been a *Capellmeister*, and at

the Thomasschule he would have to undertake
the teaching of other subjects than music, such
as Latin and grammar. He had also to promise
that he would lead a " sober and secluded life,"
set a " bright and good example " to the boys,
show the Council all respect, and not leave the
town without the express permission of the *Bürger-meister*. He was also warned that his music must
be " *nicht theatralisch*." It all has a curious air
now—these little town councillors trying to
control one of the Immortals with their petty
rules. But to Bach himself it appeared quite
normal, and he felt that the advantages of the
post outweighed the disadvantages. He was
stepping again into the full stream of life after his
seclusion in a quiet backwater ; he would once
again have the service of his own Lutheran faith
with all its richness, after the bleakness of the
" Reformed " religion ; he would be able to give
his growing sons a University education. These
were all considerations that would be likely to
have weighed heavily with him in making his
decision.

There exists an old print of Leipzig which
shows the town set on the plain much as it must
have looked to Bach's eyes, surrounded with
fortified walls, and, outside the walls, gardens
and lime-trees, and the slow river Pleisse. One
of the most conspicuous objects in the landscape
is the sharply sloping roof of the Thomaskirche

with its rounded cupola at one end, which juts
out of the scene as the name of its new Cantor was
to jut out from the history of the town in generations to come. Another print—to be found in
most illustrated books on Bach—shows the school
and church of St. Thomas at closer quarters, just
as they were when Bach first went there, in the
year 1723. There is the tall church, with the
funny little dormer windows in the roof, and, at
right angles to it, the white Thomasschule, with
regular rows of small windows and, again, the
dormers in the roof; both church and school
looking on to a cobbled open space in which is
set a stone fountain. The back of the Thomasschule looked on to a mill and a pleasant prom-
enade by the winding river, across which a
footbridge led to a resort called Apel's Garden.
That for the outside of Bach's final home. Research by Bach scholars has reconstructed for us
the inside of a vanished building—it was pulled
down long ago. The end of the Thomasschule
nearest the church contained the Rector's lodging,
the other end the Cantor's, the centre of the building was given up to the school, and the whole
width of the roof to the boys' dormitories. Bach
and his family had their own separate front door,
opening into a narrow passage leading to the
staircase; on this ground floor were two rooms
and a washhouse. On the floor above were two
bedrooms, looking on the church square, then

a narrow dining-room, leading into the parlour where the family gatherings and music-makings would take place, and at the side of the parlour was a small room with one window, Bach's study —his *Componierstube*—this room, which might have been held as a shrine valuable not only to the German people, but to the world, has been destroyed. The floor above contained three bed-rooms, and that was the extent of Bach's abode in Leipzig and where he housed his increasing family.

We can partly furnish those vanished rooms from the list of Bach's possessions made at his death, and it brings him a little closer to our imaginations to do so. It has been said of Beethoven, " He walks among the deep Invis-ibles," but in truth Bach is much more deeply an Invisible to us, not only by his earlier century, but by the formalities of his period and his personal silence. " No man," says Cecil Gray in his *History of Music*, " ever put more of himself into his works, yet his personality remains a complete enigma to us." Beethoven expressed his feelings with passionate freedom not only in his music, but in the most uncontrolled and revealing letters that perhaps have ever been written by a musician. To read them is to see his frowning brow, to hear the squeak of the over-driven quill—his tears and his laughter are before us. Of Bach we have a few letters, but they are mostly of a formal

and impersonal nature, written to princely personages with dedications, or they are about his
official appointments, about the defects of organs,
the lack of instruments or voices. They have the
stiffness of the time : they are addressed to the
" Most Distinguished and Honourable," to the
" Most Noble and Learned Magnificences," to
" My Most Gracious Patrons." If not stiff enough
they are stiffened with Latin—like the brocades
of the time, they will " stand alone." We find
Capellmeister or Cantor there, we do not find Bach,
except in certain faint suggestions, though a sense
of weight and solidity remains at the back of the
formalities. Parry's impression of these letters
and documents is that " they show a rather
surprising amount of practical qualities, common
sense, power of forcible statement expressed in a
quaintly clumsy style, and also a certain native
liveliness of temper." That he wrote more
personal letters than these official ones, we know,
for we have the long one he wrote to Georg
Erdmann and shorter ones he wrote to his cousin
Elias Bach—but in any case it is obvious that he
was not one of the " born " letter-writers. So it
makes him a little more " visible " if we realise
some of the things which surrounded his daily
life and endeavour to see him in his home. A
detailed—though obviously incomplete—list of
his property was made at his death. Spitta says :
" Bach allowed himself a certain luxury in the

matter of instruments ; of claviers alone he had five—or six if we include the little spinett (spinett-gen)—not counting the four he gave to his youngest son. Besides these he had a lute, two ' lautenclaviere,' a *viol da gamba*, and violins, violas, and violoncellos in such number that he could supply enough for any of the more simple kinds of concerted music."

Of personal and household possessions, he had two pairs of silver candlesticks, and three pairs of pinchbeck candlesticks ; several silver cups and a silver goblet and cover ; a large and small coffee-pot, a tea-pot and sugar basin, all in silver ; he had three silver snuff-boxes, and one of agate, set in gold. Of tinware there was one " washing-basin "—considering the size of the Bach family it must be hoped there were others of earthen-ware, easily broken and easily replaced at the great Leipzig Fairs. Bach himself had one silver Court sword, one silver-mounted stick, one pair of silver shoe-buckles, one silk coat—" somewhat worn," says the inventory—one cloth coat, and one " mourning cloak." He also had " at the wash " eleven linen shirts. Of house-furniture the list is short : a chest of drawers, a linen-press and clothes-press, six tables, seven wooden bed-steads, a dozen black leather chairs, and six other leather chairs, and one writing-table with drawers, which was doubtless the one Bach used when he was composing. He also possessed a number of theological books, which reflect his deep religious and mystical nature, as Geyer's *Time and Eternity* ; Rambach's *Reflections* and *On the Tears of Jesus* ; Müller's *Flame of Love* and *Hours of Refreshment* ; Tauler's *Sermons* ; Luther's *Works* ; Josephus' *History of the Jews* ; and Wagner's well-used *Leipziger Gesangbuch* in eight volumes. Two items not mentioned in this list, but which are known to have been in Bach's possession, are the portrait of his father, Ambrosius Bach, and the portrait of Anna Magdalena painted by Cristofori. Frau Bach's portrait has disappeared, but the portrait of Ambrosius Bach in its "*goldenen Rahmen*," became the property of his grandson, Carl Philipp Emanuel. When Dr. Burney visited Emanuel at Hamburg in the course of his musical tour through Germany, he was "conducted upstairs into a large and elegant music-room furnished with pictures, drawings, and prints of more than a hundred and fifty eminent musicians, among whom there are many Englishmen, and original portraits in oils of his father and grand-father." Possibly, Bach bestowed this portrait upon his second son on his marriage—he being the first of the family to enter matrimony.

Such was the setting of the Cantor's house in Leipzig, to which Bach came in 1723 and dwelt there until his death in 1750. On May 30, 1723, he had conducted in the Nicolaikirche at Leipzig his cantata *Die Elenden sollen essen*. In the words of a contemporary record, " The new Cantor and Collegii Musici Director, Herr Johann Sebastian Bach, who came from the Ducal Court of Cöthen, performed his first music here with great applause." Two days later he was formally inducted in the Thomasschule, and so began the twenty-seven years of unbroken labour he was to spend as Cantor in Leipzig. In the Cantor's house were born twelve of the thirteen children Anna Magdalena bore him ; in the Cantor's house he himself, following many of those children, was to die. On its material side, Bach's Leipzig life seems definitely provincial ; as Ernest Newman points out, " Even while he was alive he was the great provincial of music. That is his paradox—that this modest German provincial should be the most universal of musicians." Leipzig is lacking in the colour of Courts and the romantic natural and historical setting of such places as Eisenach and Weimar. On its spiritual and creative side, the Leipzig time of Bach's life is touched with the splendour of Eternity. As Sir Hubert Parry said : " The largeness of his conceptions came from innate promptings rather than from external influences." And again : " He was one of the composers who grew in scope and resourcefulness all his life long."

" I have had to work hard," Bach once said when asked as to the secret of his powers. Certainly at Leipzig he had to work as hard as any day labourer. The Bach household rose at five o'clock in summer time, and by candle-light at six o'clock in the winter. They had their *Mittags-essen* at ten o'clock, and supper at five in the afternoon.

At the time when Bach became Cantor the Thomasschule was in a state of decline. It was a thirteenth-century Augustinian foundation, created, as Gesner said, " to be a seminary of music, whereby the singing in all our churches might be provided." But for many years before Bach arrived the Thomasschule had been slowly lessening in repute and therefore in the number of its scholars. Even for the lessened number the school buildings gave inadequate accommodation —there was overcrowding, ill health, dirt. The boys—whose duty it was to supply music each Sunday in four Leipzig churches : the Thomas-kirche, the Nicolaikirche, and the less important Peterskirche and the Neukirche—were undisci-plined. The Rector, the Conrector, the Cantor, the ecclesiastical authorities and the Leipzig Town Council, seemed constantly to be in disagreement. Into all the complicated details of the quarrels it is not possible—nor would it be very enlivening— to enter here. That Bach, his mind filled with heavenly music, should have been plunged for years into all this seems in the highest degree regrettable. But Bach was no worn and fading idealist, incapable of fighting his own battles,

and we have a distinct and quite authentic vision
of him, the substantial Herr Cantor, with broad
shoulders and obstinate jaw, pushing his way
with determination through all the contumacious
crowd. Dr. Schweitzer makes the suggestion :
" We cannot say that Bach suffered from this
tension. It ministered admirably to his own need
for independence, for he played the Consistory
off against the Council and the Council against
the Consistory, and meanwhile did what he
liked." That may be regarded as a somewhat
optimistic way of looking at it. In spite of his
obstinacy, his fighting spirit, his temper, which
could flare up hotly at times, Bach's music shows
plainly his inner sensitiveness, and he must have
suffered in many ways from the strain and the
tension. After the disagreements, it is pleasant to
turn to the domestic peace of which he gives a
picture in one of those few personal letters which
have survived, the letter he wrote to the friend of
his schooldays, Georg Erdmann, when he had
been seven years in his post as Cantor. The
translation is Dr. Sanford Terry's :

" I must tell you something of my domestic
circumstances. My first wife died at Cöthen and
I have married again. Of my first marriage are
living three sons and a daughter, whom your
Honour saw at Weimar and may be pleased to
remember. Of my second marriage one son and
two daughters are living. My eldest son is a

studiosus juris, the other two are at school here in the *prima* and *secunda classis* ; my eldest daughter as yet is unmarried. My children by my second wife are still young ; the eldest boy is six. All my children are born *musici* ; from my own *familie*, I assure you, I can arrange a concert *vocaliter* and *instrumentaliter* ; my wife, in particular, has a very clear soprano, and my eldest daughter can give a good account of herself too."

But these pleasant domestic concerts, on which the candle-light of a long-past day seems to shine softly, as we imagine Bach surrounded by his singing family, his own hands drawing music from harpsichord or viola, belonged to the evening times of leisure when the work and troubles of the day were shut out.

Of that work it is time to give some account. Bach had certain purely scholastic duties, as teaching Latin, and supervising in the school during certain hours of the day—later on he paid someone else to undertake the Latin lessons in his stead. But his principal duties were supervising the four choirs for the churches, and himself training the two principal ones, the boys of which also, in accordance with ancient custom, " promenaded " singing through the streets at certain seasons. The Cantor had to accompany these processions and maintain order and good behaviour, and also on the occasions when the choirs sang at weddings and funerals. He also had to direct the music in the churches and inspect their organs. Above all he had to compose and conduct cantatas for the Sundays and Feast Days of the ecclesiastical year. Far the greater number of Bach's cantatas were written at Leipzig—in all he is supposed to have written two hundred and ninety-five cantatas, of which ninety-three have unhappily been lost, and of these roughly two hundred and sixty-five were written at Leipzig. His son Emanuel stated that his father had composed five separate cantatas for each Sunday and Festival of the ecclesiastical year. Leipzig was less impressed with these cantatas than it might earlier have been, as for years the town had fallen under the spell of operatic music. The Cantor's means of performing his cantatas were reduced to the lowest ebb as all the boys with the best voices were eager to sing in opera, and Bach was left with the poor, hoarse voices, inadequate in number at that, and a collection of musical instruments of whose deficiencies he had much cause to complain.

It is interesting for a moment to consider what was the hire of this labourer in the musical vineyard. He had his residence in the Thomasschule free of rent, he had also, in kind, sixteen bushels of corn, two cords of fire-logs, and six measures of wine. His fixed stipend was only a hundred thalers—amounting to £15 yearly—but other, though fluctuating, sources brought it

up to about £106 per annum. In the letter to
Erdmann, previously quoted, Bach had something
to say about this, after he had been Cantor for
seven years and knew well the conditions of
which he was speaking. He told his friend how he
came to Leipzig, having had " such *favourable*
reports of the *situation*," and being anxious to
obtain a good education for his sons. " But
unfortunately I have discovered," he goes on,
" that (1) this situation is not as good as it was
represented to be ; (2) various *accidentia* relative
to my *station* have been withdrawn ; (3) living is
expensive, and (4) my masters are strange folk
with very little care for music in them. Consequently I am subjected to constant annoyance,
jealousy, and persecution. . . . My present station
is worth about 700 thalers a year, and if the
death-rate is higher than *ordinairement* my *accidentia*
increase in *proportion* ; but Leipzig is a healthy
place, and for the past year, as it happens, I have
received about 100 kronen less than usual in
funeral *accidentia*. The cost of living, too, is so
excessive that I was better off in Thuringia on
400 thalers."

In another part of this letter, Bach spoke of
leaving Leipzig and trying, " with God's assistance, to seek my *fortune* elsewhere," and en-
quired if there was any suitable post at Danzig,
where Erdmann then was. But he never made
any move from Leipzig and continued to teach

and write cantatas there to the end of his days.

The Leipzig Sunday-morning service—*Haupt-gottesdienst*—in the two principal churches under Bach's control, the Thomaskirche and the Nicolaikirche, had a regular place for the cantata, each church hearing it alternatively, when the Cantor, with his *Chorus Primus*, attended to perform it. In the Thomaskirche, he directed it from the organ-loft, which was at the western end. In the Leipzig *Geistliches Gesang-Buch* of 1710 there is a quaint picture of this organ-loft and its singers and bewigged musicians playing stringed instruments and timpani ; the organist, much overweighted with wig, perched precariously on the organ-stool, the cloaked Cantor in the foreground beating time with a roll of music. The Cantor of this picture is actually Kuhnan, Bach's immediate predecessor.

The service was an elaborate one. " At six a.m. the three bells of St. Thomas' are rung. At seven candles are set out on the altar." The service began at that hour and lasted till about midday. The length of the service gives a rather sharp point to one of the rules laid down for the Thomaner boys : " Food may not be taken into church," and hardship is also revealed in the permission granted to the younger boys to return to the school-house to hear a sermon read " if the Inspector declares the cold in church beyond their endurance."

The general order of the service was this : Organ Prelude, Motet, Introit, Kyrie, Gloria, Latin Collect, Epistle, Hymn, Gospel, Credo in Latin, Prelude, followed by a Cantata, which lasted about twenty minutes, then the Creed sung in German by the congregation, Sermon lasting an hour, Hymn or second part of the Cantata, Lord's Prayer, Communion Service, Benediction. It is necessary to have this slight idea of the Lutheran service in order to realise how remains of the pre-Reformation Mass were embedded in it. Bach's B minor Mass was no sudden jump into an unknown liturgy. As Dr. Sanford Terry says in *Bach : the Historical Approach* : " The fact is not generally understood that Bach's Magnificat, settings of the ' Sanctus,' ' Kyrie,' and ' Gloria,' even the ' Benedictus ' and ' Agnus Dei ' of the Mass in B minor, were relevant to the Leipzig service." It will be seen that music had an important place in this elaborate service, and when the quality of the cantatas Bach wrote during a long sequence of years for performance at the Leipzig *Hauptgottesdienst* is recalled, the people of Leipzig must be regarded as blessed beyond their deserts in having such a Cantor. Certainly beyond their deserts. They grudged him adequate instruments and adequate voices— it seems only too certain that Bach never heard any of his Leipzig cantatas or his great Passion music really well performed—they tried to reduce

his position and his perquisites. They found
fault with him because he was not a very good
schoolmaster, and apparently had not even the
shadow of an idea that he was the most glorious
Cantor Germany has ever produced. The cantatas he wrote in his first year at Leipzig should
alone have been enough to open the eyes of the
blind and unseal the ears of the deaf, were it not
for that common human failing—inability to
recognise genius while it is actually living and
breathing, eating earthly food, and wearing out
shoe-leather. Bach's first Christmas Day at the
Thomaskirche saw the production of his Latin
Magnificat, and each of the three days of the
Christmas Festival was graced by a new cantata
from his pen. Earlier in the year, for a Leipzig
funeral, he had written his lovely motet, *Jesu,
meine Freude*. The year 1724 was equally rich,
and thereafter, year by year, Bach continued to
pour out the music within him, which issued as
from an inexhaustible fountain. It was a fountain
fed from deep sources—his Thuringian musical
ancestry, his own deep nature. As we look into
those clear and lovely waters we may well think
little of the stinging insects on the surface. But
they were there, and no account of Bach's life
can quite ignore them.

At the beginning of his cantorship, Bach
inherited, as it were, from his predecessor a
quarrel concerning his association with the music

of the University church. Bach, who was firm in upholding the honour and privileges of his post, had no mind to submit to imposition from a conceited and far from competent organist like Görner—who was one of the principal people involved in this business—and lodged a strong protest with the Council. " Not yet aware of the dogged character of its petitioner," says Dr. Sanford Terry, the Council thought to silence him by telling him that it was none of his business. But Bach's pride, as well as his pocket, was touched, and he appealed to his sovereign at Dresden (which must have caused considerable surprise and annoyance to the Leipzig authorities), and stated his case so forcibly that an enquiry was ordered. The University authorities then presented their case, without letting Bach know what they had said about him, whereupon Bach demanded—and obtained—a copy of the document, which he proceeded to answer at length, with the precision and sense of detail that were characteristic of him. Eventually he obtained part, though not all, of the rights that had been taken from his post of Cantor. But it was plain that he was not a person to be lightly put on one side. As Dr. Schweitzer says : " Bach fought for his everyday life, but not for the recognition of his art and of his works."

Of the organist Görner who was concerned in this affair a tale is told that on one occasion while

he was at the organ and Bach was conducting,
he played so badly that the Cantor snatched off
his wig and flung it at him, telling him he would
have done better to be a shoemaker.

Bach's relations with the Council in many small
matters were difficult, and if he was at times
markedly obstinate, the Council descended to
wretched meannesses—they confiscated certain
fees which were really part of his unofficial salary,
and took care that he had no share in a legacy
which was left to be divided amongst the teachers
of the Thomasschule. Bach's salary was never so
high that, with his increasing family, he could be
indifferent to losing a portion of it. But in whatever way pressure was put upon him the authorities were to discover that he was a person impossible to coerce. There is a long and involved
story about the funeral music of Queen Christiane-
Eberhardine, in which Bach was again in conflict
with the University and Görner, and great efforts
were made to induce him to sign a paper admit-
ting that he was only allowed on sufferance into
the University church to perform his music. We
are told that the University clerk called at the
Cantor's abode and spent a fruitless hour
endeavouring to make Bach sign this derogatory
document. We can imagine Bach showing him
to the door with some satisfaction. We know that
on the great occasion, amid all the civic and
University dignitaries, Bach himself conducted his

music triumphantly, though he had not signed the document. On another occasion he successfully upheld his "traditional right to order the hymns." But by 1730 the tension between Bach and the Thomaner authorities had grown acute. They wanted a commonplace, jog-trot Cantor, who would do what he was told and treat them with the respect in which their souls delighted. Having got Johann Sebastian Bach, they did not know what to do with him. They complained helplessly that he was "incorrigible," they said they had a Cantor who "does nothing, refuses to explain his conduct, and neglects his singing lessons, not to mention other instances of his unsatisfactoriness." The remark about "refuses to explain his conduct" recalls the youthful obstinate Sebastian arraigned by the Arnstadt Consistorium. He was a man made much of a piece. Little these Leipzig burghers realised how posterity was going to regard their statement that Bach "does nothing"—the Bach who had already written for them innumerable cantatas, the Magnificat, the *Johannespassion*, and the deeply devotional and marvellous *Matthäuspassion*. A very curious word to apply to these works ! So the dissatisfied Council decided to reduce his salary. Bach met their charges as to his personal behaviour with silence—he did not consider it worth while to defend himself. But he could not allow them to blame him for the deficiencies of his choirs, for which he was not responsible, so he presented them with what he called " A short and much-needed statement of the requirements of church music : with some general reflections on its decline." It is a sadly revealing document, showing, as it does, the poverty of the resources which Bach had at his disposal for the perform-ance of the works he was creating. In it he speaks with a mild restraint of " the composer's desire to hear his works performed properly." That desire can have been rarely gratified. The researches of Bach scholars have made plain a fact hitherto imperfectly realised, that when Bach wrote his music, which was intended in almost all cases for immediate performance, he had to score it according to the resources to his hand at that time. When he wrote the magnificent *Matthäus-passion* the reason the Second Coro has so much less to do is because he had only his less competent *Motettenchor* to sing it—all the more difficult vocal music had to be given to his First Choir. Deep in his mind, Bach must have had the ideal choir, the ideal orchestra and soloists. But actually, as the " short and much-needed statement " shows, he had but half-trained and imperfect voices, and even so was obliged to take singing-boys from his choirs to fill the gaps in his poor orchestra, which was partly supplied by " Town Musicians," of whom he says, " Discretion forbids me to offer an opinion on their competence and musicianship."

In former times, gaps in the Thomasschule performers had been filled by the University students, who had received a small fee for their services : but the fees were no longer forthcoming, neither were the students—" for no one cares to work for nothing," says the Cantor quietly. His summing up is eloquent : he had seventeen serviceable singers, twenty not yet serviceable, seventeen who were useless.

The Leipzig council had shown how incapable they were of understanding or appreciating Bach, and the old Rector of the Thomasschule was too aged and withdrawn to support his Cantor. But Johann Heïnrich Ernesti died in 1729, and, after some delay, Matthius Gesner was appointed in his place. Gesner had known Bach in Weimar, and the friendship begun there was renewed and deepened. A much happier state of affairs began for Bach when he had a Rector who not only reformed and improved the whole condition of the School, but valued the friendship and admired the powers of his Cantor. He would come in while the singing lessons were in progress, and " listen with pleasure to the practising of a piece of church music." When Bach wished to purchase for his choir a collection of motets, Gesner procured the money from the Council. In an edition of *Fabius Quintilianus* which he edited in 1738, Gesner gave a description of Bach playing the organ and conducting which has become classic. The glories

GB

of all the lyre players, my Fabius, he says, would
seem very trivial " could you but rise from the
dead and see Bach (whom I mention because not
long ago he was my colleague in the Thomasschule at Leipzig) ; how he with both hands, and
using all his fingers,[1] plays on a keyboard which
seems to consist of many lyres in one, and may
be called the instrument of instruments, of which
the innumerable pipes are made to sound by
means of bellows ; and how he, going one way
with his hands, and another way with the utmost
celerity with his feet, elicits by his unaided skill
many of the most various passages, which, however, uniting, produce as it were hosts of har-
monious sounds." Then he gives the picture of
Bach conducting, " presiding over thirty or forty
performers all at once, recalling this one by a nod,
another by a stamp of the foot, another with a
warning finger, keeping time and tune . . . this
one man, standing alone in the midst of the loud
sounds, having the hardest task of all, can discern
at every moment if any one goes astray, and can
keep all the musicians in order, restore any
waverer to certainty and prevent him from going
wrong ; rhythm is in his every limb, he takes in
all the harmonies by his subtle ear, as it were
uttering all the different parts through the me-
dium of his own mouth. Great admirer as I am

---

[1] Bach was one of the first to play with curved instead of flat
hand and make use of the thumb and little finger on the keyboard.

of antiquity in other respects, I yet deem this Bach of mine . . . to combine in himself many Orpheuses and twenty Arions."

It is not only a vivid little description—showing a glimpse, incidentally, of the unskilful orchestras Bach had to handle—but it displays something of Gesner's own nature. His portrait shows him sensitive, kindly, scholarly-looking, grave, but with a hint of gentle humour behind the gravity. "Together with a vast store of practical learning," Spitta says, "he possessed in an eminent degree the power of governing ; resolute firmness was combined in his character with humanity and gentleness." He greatly improved the discipline and conditions at the Thomasschule, and it was owing to his energy that extensive alterations to the actual building—overcrowded and insanitary as it had become—were undertaken. At the beginning of 1731, the entire roof was lifted and two more storeys inserted. While this operation was taking place, Bach and his family, as well as the rest of the school, were moved to temporary quarters—which in Bach's case are believed to have been in the Hainstrasse. When the Thomasschule was reopened—with speeches and celebrations—in June 1732, Bach returned there to his old unaltered abode. The additional floors were entirely for the use of the School. And so the Thomasschule stood without any further change from that date till 1877, when the building which

had sheltered Bach for twenty-seven years, the
house in which he had lived and worked and
finally died, was pulled to the ground and not
one stone left upon another. In that vanished
Componierstube of his, Bach had written the greater
number of his cantatas, both the sacred ones and
the delightful secular *Phœbus and Pan* and the
Coffee Cantata. One of the few faults that has been
found with Bach's cantatas is the complaint that
he wrote instrumentally for voices. In answer to
this, he might have said, as Beethoven did later,
" I always hear my music on instruments, never
on voices." And in the words of Professor D. F.
Tovey, " Bach writes with scrupulous attention to
the technique of every instrument known to him ;
on the principle, however, not that music is written for instruments, but that instruments (including the human voice) are made for music."

The *Johannespassion* was not written at Leipzig,
though first performed there. But the *Matthäuspassion* was created under that vanished roof of
the Thomasschule. It has taken many generations to see the true proportions of these works,
to see, as Cecil Gray says, " the Passions of Bach
. . . are a musical interpretation not only of the
events but of the inner spirit of the New Testa-
ment : he recreates in tone the personality and
acts of Christ as it had never been done before
and never has been done since by any musician."
Leipzig first heard the *Matthäuspassion* in 1729.

In a few short years that magnificent work was followed by the Mass in B minor—" better suited to the heavenly hosts than to the poor mortals to whom Bach was beholden," in Professor D. F. Tovey's opinion. So did Bach's genius maintain itself unharmed in that provincial air, surrounded in his daily life by all the noise and hurry of a big boys' school. Small leisure and less peace—a prolonged quarrel has to be detailed in the next chapter—appeared to be his portion during a considerable part of his years at Leipzig. Yet he continued to produce his music, year after year, with the same punctuality as the day dawned upon the old Thomasschule.

CHAPTER V

UNFORTUNATELY for Bach's content Matthias Gesner only remained Rector of the Thomasschule for four years. Then he was called to the University at Göttingen and the Conrector Johann August Ernesti was appointed in his place. Unlike the earlier Ernesti who was Rector when Bach first went to Leipzig, the second Ernesti was to prove a thorn in the flesh and the cause of many harassments to the Cantor. Bach was now forty-nine years old, well into middle age, beginning almost certainly to feel the strain of his life of teaching and unceasing creative work. His great gift had brought him, as has been said, few honours, and but the most moderate worldly competence. The Frau Cantorin, so thriftily running Bach's household and bearing and bringing up those of their children who survived infancy, can have had few spare thalers. Thrifty though the Herr Cantor had need to be, he was also hospitable, and few distinguished musicians came to Leipzig who did not pay their respects to him and receive some entertainment. When he himself was not well enough to go to Handel, at a time when he was visiting Saxony, he sent a special invitation to his great contemporary. But Handel, apparently, never realised Bach's existence as a matter of any interest to him.

The new Rector, Ernesti, had apparently no more imagination with regard to Bach than had Handel. He was twenty-two years younger than the Cantor, but not even the respect due to a much older man than himself seems to have softened the acerbity of his behaviour when things went wrong. It is difficult for posterity to regard with patience the spectacle of Bach, irritable and obstinate though he undoubtedly could be at times, harried and baited by younger men who are only rescued from their natural oblivion because they behaved ill to one so incomparably greater than themselves.

Ernesti no doubt felt that to become Rector of the Thomasschule at the age of twenty-seven was an achievement. He was capable and well-qualified ; he was a " new broom " who was going to sweep away all antiquated ideas, and to his self-satisfied mind the Herr Cantor represented a passing, if not past, generation. He thought they had outgrown Bach, not realising that to him and others like him Bach was not even " visible." Apart from his temperament, Ernesti was the less fitted to understand Bach, as he definitely despised

music and did not regard it as part of a serious
education at all. Instead of, like Gesner, coming
in and listening with pleasure to the music
practisings, if he found a youth engaged in
improving his skill on an instrument, he would
make the sneering remark, " So, you mean to be
a pot-house fiddler ! " As though music had no
place save at the doors of taverns. A strange
remark under the roof that sheltered Bach, and
a roof, moreover, that had been built many years
before Bach was born, for the very purpose of
training and teaching church musicians. Bach
was not likely to submit tamely to such a funda-
mental heresy. Here were all the elements of
conflict, which soon arose over two of the school
prefects, both, somewhat awkwardly, named
Krause. The first Krause, Gottfried Theodor,
was a young man of twenty-two, of whom Bach
had such a high opinion that he made him head
prefect of his *Chorus Primus*, and gave him power
to keep order during the church singing, and, if
necessary, to punish the smaller and unruly boys
in the Cantor's absence. The choir evidently took
advantage of the young prefect, and, in spite of
admonition and warning, behaved so ill that
Krause took up the rod, and, in the general excitement, apparently used it rather heavily. At least
one of the boys complained that he was cut and
bleeding, though investigation revealed no signs
of a broken skin. But the tale, doubtless with

trimmings, was carried to Ernesti, who, to the astonishment of everyone, ordered that Krause should be publicly thrashed before the whole school. Krause's school career had been exemplary, and he was not only first prefect, but a grown-up young man on the point of going to the University : such a punishment would have spread far beyond the precincts of the Thomas-schule and marked his future career. Krause flung himself on Bach's protection, who thereupon pleaded for him with the Rector and took the blame on his own shoulders for having given Krause authority to punish. But the Rector would listen to no reason and no appeal—he was, under cover of Krause, undermining the Cantor's authority, and Bach knew this quite well. Krause then asked to be given his certificate—" Dimission "—and allowed to leave the school. This also Ernesti refused—he was determined on his pound of flesh—and, to avoid public humiliation, Krause simply fled from Leipzig and all his future prospects. Ernesti even descended to the meanness of keeping back Krause's belongings and thirty thalers standing to his account in the school funds.

When Krause thus disappeared, the Second Choir prefect also bore the name of Krause, Johann Krause, son of a miller. Unlike Gottfried Theodor, the character of Johann was bad—Bach once called him " a disreputable dog "—and

Ernesti had, earlier, agreed with Bach's verdict. But Johann Krause had a seniority which demanded consideration, though as second prefect he had been inefficient and unsatisfactory, and he was also of so little worth musically that Bach naturally objected when Ernesti promoted him to be first prefect in the place of his departed namesake. Still he put up with this till Krause proved himself so unsatisfactory that Bach deposed him again to second prefect, and put the third prefect in his place. He told Ernesti that he had done this and his reasons for doing it. Krause appealed to the Rector ; the Rector sent him to the Cantor with his complaints, and Bach, in a fit of natural, if unwise, anger, told Krause that he had deposed him on purpose to show the Rector who was master of the music at the Thomasschule. Krause joyfully returned to the Rector—we see him weaving like a malicious shuttle between the Rector's and the Cantor's abodes at either end of the building—and repeated these remarks. Ernesti asked for an explanation, and Bach, in a thorough rage, repeated his words without mitigation to the Rector's face. Reflection apparently showed Bach that he had gone too far, and he agreed to meet Ernesti's wishes and restore Krause. But Krause again behaved so badly at the next practise that it was impossible to do this. Ernesti then threatened that if Bach did not reinstate the prefect, he himself would do so on the ensuing Sunday. From words the Rector and the Cantor, both by now too angry to consider wisdom or example, proceeded to action. We behold a choleric Cantor, with no gentle hand, turning Krause out of the organ-loft of the Thomasschule in the middle of the morning service. We behold the Rector appearing before vespers the same afternoon and forbidding the boys, under heavy penalties, to obey the Cantor, who shortly afterwards arrived to see Krause again in charge. Bach promptly turned him out, and then found the boys were so terrified by the Rector's threats that no one dared lead the motet. But he had his devoted pupil Krebs with him, who undertook the leadership. It is a curious and painful scene. Bach's violence was undoubtedly wrong, though his impulsive vigour has its enlivening aspect, but when it is realised that the wretched quarrel dragged on for nearly two years, it will be seen that its effects would be very injurious to Bach's position in the Thomasschule—there is extant a somewhat pathetic letter to the Leipzig Council in which he begs that the Rector may be admonished " to cease to impede me in my duties, nor by threat of punishment to prevent the *alumni* from giving me the *obedience* due to me "—and to his peace of mind as a composer. The correspondence from Bach and Ernesti to " their Magnificences " the Council still exists, and it is by this correspondence the

case must be judged, and upon that " the verdict
goes unhesitatingly to Bach : Ernesti's letters are
tinged with pettiness and spite, and his venture-
some contradiction of Bach on his own subject
suggests that he was as uninstructed in it as he
was generally self-sufficient and dogmatic."[1]

So long before these troubles as 1733, Bach had
appealed to the new King-Elector of Poland-
Saxony, asking his protection and saying that he
was suffering from " undeserved affronts which
are likely to continue " unless his position should
be improved by his appointment to the King's
Capelle. With this appeal he had sent, as an offering, the Kyrie and Gloria of the B minor Mass.
Through various causes—of which an indifference
to music in the Elector's soul may be regarded as
one, as apparently the glorious music was never
performed, and lay neglected—this appointment
was long in the granting, and it was not till the
end of 1736 that Bach could call himself *Hof-
Compositeur* to the Court at Dresden. No doubt
this distinction, which seems so trifling by the side
of his works, brought some balm to his German
heart, and would cause the Leipzig Council to
regard him with increased respect. The confer-
ring of this honour is associated with the Russian
Envoy to the Dresden Court, Count von Kayserling, who had in his employ as clavecinist a pupil of
Bach's, Gottlieb Goldberg. Count von Kayserling

[1] *Bach : a Biography*, C. Sanford Terry.

suffered acutely from insomnia and its attendant melancholy, and found music his best consoler during his sleepless nights. He commissioned Bach to write some music for Goldberg to play to him, and Bach produced the wonderful Thirty Variations which are now commonly called the " Goldberg Variations," for which he received a hundred louis d'or. The Count appreciated the lovely thing he had obtained, and never wearied of listening to the skilful fingers of Bach's pupil playing the Variations with all their manifold freshness and charm, ending up with the joyful little quodlibet—that kind of musical game the Bach clans, when they met together, were fond of enjoying.

Before this time, Bach's sons—of his first marriage—were coming to manhood. Wilhelm Friedemann, the eldest of them, and the most brilliantly gifted, was Bach's favourite, as in Friedemann he found a musical temperament akin to his own. Unfortunately, though he inherited a considerable portion of his father's musical gifts, he was lacking in the moral stamina, the strong and upright character that his father so eminently possessed. In his later years Friedemann sank to an impoverished and unsettled existence, reduced to selling some of his father's manuscripts and to pretending that manuscripts of his own were the work of his great parent. He gave organ recitals for his livelihood, and his powers of improvisation were remarkable—but he was lazy and shiftless, and willing to live a hand-to-mouth existence rather than settle down to the life of hard and steady work which so many generations of Bachs had lived. But fortunately for the pride and happiness of his father, all his worst years were after the Cantor had been laid in his grave. Friede-mann's portrait, painted in the later years of his life, shows a type of good looks not common in the Bach family—his features are aquiline, with long thin nose, a slightly sneering smile, small eyes with a curious expression ; the face of a man who might easily be fascinating, but was hardly trust-worthy. He had a beautifully shaped long-fingered hand. It can be imagined that in his young manhood he would appear full of promise and charm. It was with his eldest son that Bach used to go to Dresden to hear the opera there, saying " Well, Friedemann, shall we go over to Dresden to hear the pretty little tunes ? " In 1733, Friedemann had received the post of organist at the Sophienkirche at Dresden, which was a cause of considerable satisfaction to his father, who from his ninth year had given him his musical education, writing specially for him a *Clavierbüchlein*, and, as he advanced in musical knowledge, he wrote for this brilliant son the Little Preludes and Inventions and the first book of the *Wohltemperirte Clavier*. It is very characteristic of Bach that he should have produced this immortal

work as a lesson-book for his son Friedemann, to
be handed down later for the use of his second
son Carl Philipp Emanuel.

With Philipp Emanuel we return to the solid
Bach virtues. His portrait shows the Bach type
of square heavy face, head set well into the
shoulders, the air of determination, and evident
capacity for work. Emanuel's career was what
might be expected from his face, combined with
his inherited gifts. He attained to a worthy and
honourable position, he became cembalist to
Frederick the Great—whose royal flute-playing
it was no unmixed joy to accompany, as he took
painful liberties with *tempo* which etiquette might
not correct—and later on secured his release from
the Prussian Court and became cantor at the
Johanneum in Hamburg, where he died in his
seventy-fifth year.

Carl Philipp Emanuel Bach is of considerable
importance in the history of music, especially in
regard to clavier playing, on which he wrote his
Art das Clavier zu Spielen, setting forth his father's
principles, which from that work were developed
by Clementi, Hummel, and Cramer. Mozart
said, " He is the father, we are the children.
Those of us who can do well, have learnt from
him." Haydn gave much study to Emanuel's
compositions, and the evolution of sonata-form is
largely traced to him. Emanuel always said that
both for clavier playing and composition he had

no other teacher than his father, and, in the same
fragment of autobiography from which that statement is taken, he says that he had " from my youth
upwards enjoyed the rare good fortune to have at
home, and likewise to hear there, the most admirable of all species of music." He goes on to say
that in his youth at Leipzig " hardly any professor
of music passed through that city without making
the acquaintance of my father, and playing before
him. The grandeur of my father in composition,
and in organ and clavier playing, so peculiarly
his own, was too widely known for any musician
of note to miss the opportunity of associating, if
possible, on an intimate footing with that great
man."

After Philipp Emanuel left the service of
Frederick the Great and settled in Hamburg, he
was visited by Dr. Burney, father of the more
famous Fanny, and it is very curious to observe
how Dr. Burney laboured under the delusion that
Sebastian Bach's principal claim to remembrance
was that he was the father of the celebrated Carl
Philipp Emanuel.

To continue this brief outline of Bach's sons.
The third was Gottfried Bernhard, who was also
musically gifted and became organist at Mühlhausen and Sangerhausen, and died at the age of
twenty-four. Before his death he had got heavily
into debt and ran away from his post as organist,
his family not knowing his whereabouts. One of

the most touchingly personal of Bach's letters remaining concerns this erring son. He had paid Bernhard's debts at Mühlhausen, only to find he had fled from debts again at Sangerhausen. " What can I do or say more," the poor father wrote to Herr Klemm, with whom Bernhard had lived in Sangerhausen, " my warnings having failed, and my loving care and help having proved unavailing ? I can only bear my cares in patience and commend my undutiful boy to God's mercy, never doubting that He will hear my sorrow-stricken prayer and in His good time bring my son to understand that the path of conversion leads to Him."[1]

Of Anna Magdalena's sons who lived to grow up only two concern us, as the eldest, Gottfried Heinrich, was mentally deficient. Christoph Friedrich, the next son, was a capable musician and prolific composer, and when only eighteen obtained a Court appointment to Count Wilhelm of Schaumberg-Lippe at Bückeburg. The youngest son of Sebastian and Anna Magdalena, Johann Christian, who was to be called the " English Bach " was his father's Benjamin, for it was to him he made the present of three clavier cembali which caused some little dispute after his death. He was only fifteen when his father died, and for a time lived with his half-brother Emanuel. From there he went to Italy and studied under

[1] *Bach : a Biography*, C. Sanford Terry.

HB

Martini, becoming a Roman Catholic, and organist at Milan Cathedral. He composed not only sacred music, but operas in the Italian manner. From Italy he came to England, and was appointed music-master to Queen Caroline. When the young Mozart came to London in 1764, Christian Bach was much interested in him, and they performed together. He was associated with public concerts at Almack's and the Hanover Square Rooms. He was painted by Gainsborough and the portrait shows him handsome, assured, elegant with lace ruffles and ringed finger. " The careers of his brothers, by comparison," says Dr. Sanford Terry, " were commonplace, his father's reputation provincial." This last son of the great Cantor walked about Soho and the Haymarket, went to Vauxhall, and for a time lived at Richmond. He even attained the distinction of being noticed by Dr. Johnson, who asked Burney, " Pray, sir, who is Bach ? Is he a piper ? " An ignorance somewhat strange considering Christian Bach's importance in the life of his day in London. He died in 1782, and was buried in London. He was married to an Italian opera singer, but had no children. The patriarchal families of the Bachs ceased with Sebastian himself, but Dr. Sanford Terry's researches have proved that it was not till May 1871 that in direct descent " Bach's blood has ceased to flow in mortal veins."

But the careers of all these musicians gain their principal interest to us because they were the sons of the great Johann Sebastian, and to him it is time to return. He never set foot outside his native Germany, and in Germany his travels were almost confined to Thuringia and Saxony—his widest range outside these two kingdoms taking him to Hamburg and Berlin. But his mind ranged where his foot never went, and his increasing age brought no decline in his powers. The long-protracted quarrel with Ernesti over the prefects at last faded away when the King-Elector responded to his *Hof-Compositeur's* appeal to " release me from certain provocations that weigh upon me." The marriage of Princess Amelia in the spring of 1738, with its accompanying festivities and *Abend-Musik* provided by Bach and performed by the University students in the Marktplatz, set the seal on Bach's position, and made Ernesti realise that his Cantor would have in future to be treated with more consideration and respect.

Such other attacks as Bach suffered from were caused by petty outside jealousies, like that of Scheibe, an unsuccessful organist, in 1737. The amusing thing about this attack is that Scheibe is reduced to finding fault in such a way that his missile turns round and becomes praise. He says that Bach's " music is exceedingly difficult to play, because the efficiency of his own limbs sets his standard ; he expects singers and players to be as agile with voice and instrument as he is with his fingers, which is impossible." Again, he complains, " All his parts, too, are equally melodic, so that one cannot distinguish the principal tune among them." A remark that might well cause the student in counterpoint, struggling with his wooden " inner parts," to tear his hair, and surely must have made Bach himself smile.

The last decade of Bach's life offers few striking incidents. His industry continued, and the year 1744 was made memorable by the completion of the second half of the 48 Preludes and Fugues commonly known together as the *Well-tempered Clavier.* Twenty-two years elapsed between the first and second portions of this work, which has remained a perpetual joy to all musicians since its creation. Its freshness and its maturity, its depth and its beauty, its response to all moods, make it incomparable in the whole realm of music. In miniature, as it were, in " The 48 " we see what is true of the great mass of Bach's music, how universal he is. He provides the whole range of human food. He is good sound bread and butter, he is beef and beer—or its German equivalent—he is honey from the comb, and he is that something mysterious when food ceases to be food and becomes a sacrament, when the bread is no longer bread, and the wine more than the juice of the grape.

Bach had written cantatas from the year 1704, when he was nineteen years old, to 1744, when he was fifty-nine. " But this surprising record of official duty shows no sign of flagging, of perfunctory approach, of jaded effort. It declares, rather, the unplumbable resources of his genius ; for no limits to his inventiveness appear. Till the very end the well of his inspiration yielded its waters with generous spontaneity, and melodies of the most fragrant beauty flowed at his easy command."[1] Well might Picander, whose texts Bach often used in his Leipzig cantatas, say that the defects of his verse would be made good " by the loveliness of the music of our incomparable *Capellmeister* Bach." It is not only musical genius but religious devotion that created these cantatas, the scores of which were headed " Jesu, help me ! " and ended with the words " To God alone the praise." Throughout his life that was the spirit in which Bach worked.

We are fortunate in having several portraits of Bach. The best known—as most often reproduced—is the portrait that was painted when he was elected to Mizler's Musical Society in 1747. One of the conditions of membership was that a portrait should be presented, as well as an original composition. The heavy face, the broad nose, slightly on one side, as was his father's, the thick eyebrows shielding the eyes so obviously weakened

[1] *The Music of Bach*, C. Sanford Terry.

and drawn together by over-much use, the little
frown obviously caused more by defective sight
than temper, the genial mouth, the massive
forehead, the grey wig, the broad shoulders,
and the curiously chubby hand holding the
" *Canon triplex à 6 voc.*," are all made familiar to
us by Haussmann's brush. It is interesting to
compare that portrait with the one by Jakob Ihle,
hanging in the Bach Museum at Eisenach,
painted when Bach was thirty-five. The chin is
less heavy, the eyes are much larger, and have a
deep mystical look that agrees with so much of
his music. There is also an unusual contemporary
drawing of Bach which was in the possession of a
Leipzig family during his lifetime—it is reproduced in Dr. Sanford Terry's *Origin of the Family
of Bach Musicians*. It is a very human Bach we see
there, his hand tucked into his unbuttoned waist-
coat, his wig pushed a little back, the curves of
his mouth full of good temper, the characteristic
little frown hardly visible—but the eyes have a
strange remote stare, as if he was looking at things
unseen.

Bach, it has been said, preferred playing the
viola in chamber music, for then he felt himself
" in the middle of the harmony." His life may
be regarded as an exact instance of the middle way
of fortune. He sprang from the middle class ;
he knew neither extreme poverty nor wealth ; he
experienced the normal joys and griefs of life—he

was early left an orphan ; he lost his first wife and many children ; he had one son who was mentally defective and another who was a spendthrift and ne'er-do-weel. His path at times was thorny with difficulties—not the great tragedies which befall some, but those little daily stabs and distresses which taken together can produce a considerable sum of suffering. On the other hand he had the companionship for twenty-eight years of a wife who was a real helpmate, a girl who grew to maturity at his side—Anna Magdalena, of whom faint surviving voices give an impression of sweetness. In the later years a cousin, Elias Bach, came to live in the Cantor's house at Leipzig, as tutor to his younger children, and his letters give an idea of Bach's household—" A rare glimpse," as Dr. Sanford Terry says, " into an interior otherwise dimly visible." These letters were published in *Die Musik*, and the following quotations are taken from Dr. Sanford Terry's translation. Elias Bach lived with the Cantor at Leipzig from 1738 to 1742, and his letters give the picture of a busy and affectionate household. Anna Magdalena he calls " unsere Frau Muhme," and his admiration for, and devotion to, Bach, whom he refers to as " our dear Herr Papa," are evident. He requests that from his home may be sent some measures of muscat wine, " to give our Cousin pleasure, in return for the many benefits I have received in his home these two years past." There are some charming little glimpses as to the tastes of the Frau Cantorin : " I should like to give some yellow carnations to our Frau Muhme ! " Elias writes to his mother, " she loves the garden and would be so pleased to have them." When the plants arrive, he tells how delighted she is with them, they " have given her more pleasure even than children find in their Christmas gifts ; she nurtures them as tenderly as a child lest harm befall them." Through these letters we also have a little glimpse of Bach making enquiries as to a singing linnet he had heard at Halle. " Frau Muhme is very fond of linnets," says Elias. Not content with all the music they made among themselves, the Bach family apparently delighted in singing-birds—thus linking themselves to Mozart and that starling of his which he first heard singing in a bird-shop the Allegretto theme of his G Major Concerto.

Another very human little touch we get from these letters. Elias had been requested by his stepbrother for the loan of one of Bach's cantatas, and Elias had to refuse, as the parts were already in the hands of a borrower who had not returned them, and Bach will not " allow the score out of his hands, for he has lost several by lending them to other people."

From this quiet home of his, Bach had been in the habit of making short journeys, most frequently in the autumn, to visit different musical

centres, to play on good organs or conduct a
cantata. These were his only holidays—there
were no formal vacations at the Thomasschule
for either pupils or teachers, a week of half-
holidays in the dog-days or a holiday in celebra-
tion of the " Name-day " of one of the masters
were all they received, otherwise the work went
on unbroken throughout the year. Bach had been
bound, on his appointment as Cantor, to promise
not to leave Leipzig without the express permission
of the *Bürgemeister*. In his later years at any rate,
this rule apparently was not much enforced. On
one of these occasions he visited Dresden, in
September 1731, partly to hear Hasse's opera
Cleofide, and partly to give an organ recital in the
Sophienkirche. This recital was attended by
Hasse and all the important musicians of Dresden,
and moved a local poet to compare Bach to
Orpheus, maintaining that the god's classic lute
was far less magical than Bach's " nimble hand,"
which charmed not mere dumb beasts, but filled
the hearts of grown men with wonder.

In the following autumn, Bach went to Cassel—
where, many years earlier, he had played to the
Prince, who pulled the ring from his finger and
bestowed it upon him. This time he was accompanied by Anna Magdalena—a proud and happy
woman, it may be imagined—and it was his
business to examine and report on the recently
enlarged organ of the Martinskirche. He spent

a week over the organ, and, on the second Sunday of his stay, gave a public recital upon it, which caused great satisfaction to the people of Cassel. They treated him and his wife with handsome consideration, accommodating them at the Stadt Stockholm at a cost of eighty-four thalers, providing porters to carry them to and fro when they went out, and a special servant to look after them, as well as a fee of fifty thalers and twenty-six thalers for the expenses of the journey.

The most famous of Bach's visits is that he paid to Frederick the Great in 1747. Since 1740, Carl Philipp Emanuel Bach had been cembalist at the Prussian Court, other members of which knew Bach or had been his pupils—Frederick inevitably had heard talk of the great Leipzig Cantor, and his curiosity had been aroused. He gave Carl Philipp several indications that his father's presence would be welcomed at Potsdam. Carl Philipp had married in 1744—the first marriage in the family—and in 1745 an infant was born who was Bach's first grandchild. It was to see his daughter-in-law and grandson that Bach at last travelled to Berlin, and thus came into touch with Frederick the Great. Friedemann accompanied him, and Forkel says, " often told me the story." Forkel goes on, " Nor am I likely to forget the racy manner in which he related it. The courtesy of those days demanded rather prolix compliments, and the first introduction of Bach to so illustrious a monarch, into whose presence he had hurried without being allowed time to change his travelling dress for a cantor's black gown, obviously invited ceremonial speeches on both sides."

The King amused his leisure with concerts, in which he played to his own, and no doubt to his Court's, satisfaction many flute concertos. On this occasion the scene was set, the attendant band waiting on their master, who was adjusting his flute, when a list of the new arrivals was handed to him, which he glanced at, and then exclaimed, with some excitement, " Gentlemen, Old Bach has arrived ! "

We have Dr. Burney's account of the King's concert-room at the Palace of Potsdam, ornamented with immense mirrors and gilt and green sculptures, one of the new Silbermann Hammer-claviers " beautifully varnished and embellished," and, for the use of the royal flautist, a tortoisc-shell music-desk " richly and elegantly inlaid with silver." Tortoise-shell and silver were evidently to Frederick's taste, for in another apartment of the palace was a harpsichord by Shudi, made in England, the frame, hinges, and pedal all of silver, the front of tortoise-shell, and the case inlaid.

Into this magnificence was ushered the travel-stained " Old Bach." The King abandoned his flute concerto for the evening, and invited his

honoured visitor to try the various Silbermann
fortepianos, of which he had a large collection,
that stood about the Palace apartments. " Accompanied from room to room by the King and
the musicians," Forkel continues, " Bach tried
the instruments and improvised upon them before
his illustrious companion. After some time he
asked the King to give him a subject for a fugue,
that he might treat it extempore. The King did
so, and expressed his astonishment at Bach's pro-
found skill in developing it. Anxious to see to
what lengths the art could be carried, the King
desired Bach to improvise a six-part fugue. But
as every subject is not suitable for polyphonic
treatment, Bach himself chose a theme, and, to
the astonishment of all who were present,
developed it with the skill and distinction he had
shown in treating the King's subject."

When he returned home, Bach developed the
royal theme into the work which he called a
Musicalisches Opfer, and sent it to Frederick the
Great with the flattering epistle which sovereigns
expected from subjects in those days. Though
we feel the praise is pitched too high when he
tells the King that the most distinguishing part of
the " Musical Offering " is " the work of your
Majesty's own illustrious hand," and that it was
because he felt his impromptu development of the
theme had not been worthy of its excellence he
had developed it more fully in the " Offering "—

in spite of the ornateness of phrase we feel that
Bach was conscious of his own worth and the
quality of his work. Court etiquette in the
eighteenth century was formal, but Bach was not
a person at any time to be dazzled by false values,
and still less so at the age of sixty-two as he
was when he had his meeting with Frederick the
Great.

A month after his return from Berlin, Bach
consented to become a member of Mizler's Society
for the Promotion of Musical Science, to which
Handel already belonged, and presented the
society with his wonderful Canonic Variations on
the Christmas melody *Vom Himmel hoch*, of which
Spitta says, " the work has an element of solemn
thankfulness, like the gaze of an old man who
watches his grandchildren standing round their
Christmas-tree, and is reminded of his own child-
hood." He was also engaged on his great work
Die Kunst der Fuge, whose importance and beauty
is only now beginning to be realised. In it the
" Old father of Fugues " spoke his last word in
that form so linked with his name. He loved
fugues because he loved order—the chaotic and
unfinished was against his grain. And the order
that rules his music is the same order that controls
the placing of the stars and the feathers in a bird's
beautiful wing—it is essential and eternal. And
Bach had attained to such freedom and mastery
within the form that he could step outside the

laws without destroying the spirit which ruled them. It is because of this that there is such essential unity in all his works—the smallest things he writes, simple almost as the chirp of a bird just out of the egg, are not unworthy to march in the company of the things that make our hearts stand still by their depth and majesty. We feel the truth of the words of one of Bach's German biographers : " He is one of those rare personalities that do not become, but always are." It sounds a little like the Athanasian Creed ; nevertheless, it shows real insight into that character at once so simple and so complex.

In January 1749 the second wedding among Bach's children took place. Carl Philipp Emanuel had married in Berlin, but Elisabeth Juliane Friederica, the eldest of Anna Magdalena's three living daughters, was married from her father's house : she would only have to walk across the cobbled church square to the Thomaskirche for the ceremony. We can imagine that Bach felt content as he took his Lissgen, as he called her, on his arm to church, for the man she was marrying, Johann Christoph Altnikol, had been a pupil of his own—" a dear former pupil " he had named him in one of his letters—and at the time of his marriage was organist of the Wengelskirche at Naumburg, a post for which he was indebted to his father-in-law. Bach lived to see a son born of this marriage, who was christened

Johann Sebastian, but did not live quite so long as his grandfather.

Bach was blessed with the sturdy health of his Thuringian forbears, for during the whole of his life he appears to have worked with unflagging vigour. He seems to have only once been laid by for a time, either with illness or an accident. But the summer after his daughter's marriage signs of failing health showed themselves—so markedly that with unsympathetic haste the Leipzig authorities began to make arrangements to appoint his successor. Bach's eyesight, used unceasingly almost since his infancy in the writing of musical scores, began at last to give way. It became so bad that resort was had to operation at the hands of an English oculist then travelling in Germany. The unhappy result was complete blindness. While he had still been able to see, Bach had been revising his Eighteen Choral Preludes for the Organ, and had written out with his own hand fifteen of them. Then the darkness descended, when his hand could no longer work. He knew death was near, but he had never shrunk from the thought of death ; all through his life that thought had been to him a deep consolation, an inspiration to some of his loveliest and most tender music. He had done his work and was prepared to depart, but first there was one small thing to finish. He summoned his son-in-law Altnikol, who was particularly sympathetic to

him, and also his dear Lissgen, who was mourning
her little son, the small Johann Sebastian, who
had just died. They came, and, by the bedside of
the dying Cantor, Altnikol sat him down, pen in
hand, to write at his dictation the last notes that
were to come from the mind of Sebastian Bach.
He wrote out the Choral Preludes *Jesus Christus
unser Heiland* and *Komm Gott*—these were the sixteenth and the seventeenth. There remained the
last, the eighteenth, the organ Prelude he had
made on the hymn *Wenn wir in höchsten Nöthen
seien*—" When we are in deepest need." But
Bach was past his deepest need ; his earthly life
was done. Another hymn came to his mind, and
he bade Altnikol to use instead the words " *Vor
deinen Thron tret ich hiemit* " :

> *Before Thy Throne, my God I stand,*
> *Myself, my all, are in Thy hand ;*
> *Turn to me Thine approving face,*
> *Nor from me now withhold Thy grace.*

The score, in Altnikol's handwriting, ends in
the middle of the twenty-sixth bar—Bach had
dictated his last note. He lived just a little longer,
and for a short time before his death his sight
suddenly returned to him. In the words of the
Nekrolog : " Ten days before his death his eyes
seemed to improve, so that once in the morning
he could see quite well and also bear the light

again." It was but one last glimpse he was given of the faces of his family and his wife. Many years earlier, when she was a bride, he had written a song in her *Notenbüchlein* :

> *If thou art with me, I would gladly go*
> *To death and to my rest.*
> *Ah, how contented would be my end*
> *If thy tender hands would close*
> *My faithful eyes.*

She was with him. After this last glimpse of the world, he was smitten into unconsciousness with apoplexy, and for ten days lingered in a high fever. He died in the evening of Tuesday, July 28, 1750. On the Friday of that week he was buried in the churchyard of the Johanniskirche, outside the walls of Leipzig. No monument was raised to his memory. Leipzig quickly forgot her greatest citizen. His goods were distributed among his children. His widow was permitted to receive the Cantor's salary for half a year after his decease on consideration of giving up her quarters at the Thomasschule. She was allowed to sink into poverty—there is pathetic record of her being reduced to selling her husband's manuscripts— both by her stepsons and the town of Leipzig. At her death, ten years after Bach's, she was an alms-woman, and was buried as a pauper. One by one, as the eighteenth century drew to its close

Iв

Bach's sons and daughters died. In 1800 only Regine Susanna was living, and she was so poor that Rochlitz issued an appeal on her behalf: " The Bach family is now extinct except one single daughter of the great Sebastian Bach ; and this daughter, now advanced in years, is in want. Very few know this fact, for she cannot—no, she must not, shall not, beg ! " Beethoven responded to this appeal, or a second one for the daughter as he called her, " of the immortal god of harmony," and, after receiving the first contributions, Susanna wrote, " If it is granted to the spirits of my father and brothers to sympathise in what befalls me, how must their past compassion be turned into joyful sympathy with my happiness ! "

.   .   .   .

As early as 1808 the English musician, Samuel Wesley, was writing ardent and enlightened letters to a friend as to the surpassing merits of the compositions of Johann Sebastian Bach—" Saint Sebastian " is his phrase. It was largely through his exertions that Forkel's Life was—very badly— first translated into English, and Wesley says : " It appears by the Life of Sebastian, he was not only the Greatest Master in the World, but also one of the most worthy and amiable Characters that ever adorned Society." Wesley could not forgive Dr. Burney, who had known and visited Bach's son, Carl Philipp Emanuel, for his failure to discern Sebastian's surpassing greatness, and the letters give an amusing picture of Wesley metaphorically forcing the aged and tottering Dr. Burney to his knees while he played to him the Preludes and Fugues, and discoursed on " the immortal and adamantine Pillars of Sebastian's Harmony." It was Wesley's daughter Eliza who bequeathed to the British Museum the precious autograph copy of the second part of the " Well-tempered Clavier."

In Germany it was Forkel who first realised the true greatness of Bach—his contemporaries had been most impressed, apparently, by his powers as an executant musician. It is not till we come to the generation of Mendelssohn and Schumann that the full light begins to dawn. Mendelssohn conducted the first performance of the *Matthäus-passion* ever heard by living ears of that time. Zelter instructed Goethe in the Bach doctrine, and told him that, could he hear a performance of one of Bach's motets at the Singakademie, he would feel himself " at the centre of the world." Mendelssohn had played to Schumann that lovely organ chorale, *Schmücke dich, O liebe Seele*, and Schumann wrote to him afterwards : " The melody seemed interlaced with garlands of gold, and the work breathed forth such happiness that you inspired in me this avowal : ' Were life deprived of all trust, of all faith, this simple chorale would restore all to me.' I fell into a reverie ; then, almost unconsciously, I found myself in the cemetery, and I felt poignant grief at not being able to cover with flowers the grave of the great Bach." On another occasion Schumann said, " Bach was a man—out and out ; with him nothing is half done, morbid ; everything is written as if for eternity." Beethoven had earlier said, making a play on the meaning of his name, " His name ought not to be Bach, but Ocean." Zelter expressed a memorable thought when he wrote of Bach, " This Leipzig Cantor is one of God's own phenomena—clear, yet never to be cleared up." The same sense of strangeness overtook Richard Wagner when he contemplated " the appearance, otherwise almost inexplicably mysterious, of the musical marvel Sebastian Bach. . . . Look at this head, hidden in its absurd French full-bottomed wig ; look at this master, a miserable cantor and organist in little Thuringian towns whose names we hardly know now, wearing himself out in poor situations, always so little considered that it needed a whole century after his death to rescue his works from oblivion."

It remained impossible to recognise Bach's full greatness till his works were published to the world. For a century and more after his death they only existed in manuscript, and in rare engraved and printed editions of certain works. One hundred years after Bach had been laid in his grave the Bachgesellschaft was formed, and proceeded through half a century to publish the complete works. From that have sprung the innumerable editions which can now be obtained. Being at last awakened to Bach's importance, the German people began to look round for his grave, that they might place a belated laurel wreath upon it. They could not find it—only a tradition said that it had been six paces from the south door of the Johanniskirche. So a tablet was placed on the south wall saying that " on this side " of the one-time churchyard had been his grave. Nearly a decade later the church was enlarged, and the demolition and digging gave an opportunity to search for the long-neglected grave—only one fact beyond the traditional position being known : that Bach was buried in an oaken coffin, which at the date of his death was unusual. After three days of digging an oak coffin was found which contained the well-preserved skeleton of a man who in age, height, and massiveness of skull corresponded with what was known of Bach's appearance. The sculptor Karl Seffner modelled a head upon a cast of the skull, and the result gave the undoubted countenance of Bach as the portraits showed it. After other investigations there was left little doubt that the mortal remains of Bach had been found, and they were reburied under the altar of the Johanniskirche, while the Leipzig University Gesangverein stood round and

sang the chorale from Bach's *Matthäuspassion* :
" When I come to die." So to his own music
were Bach's bones laid to their final rest, and the
tomb sealed over him to whom, as Schumann said,
music owes almost as much as Christianity owes
to its Founder.

BIBLIOGRAPHY

Bach : a Biography, by C. Sanford Terry. Oxford University Press.
> Absolutely indispensable to all students of Bach.

Johann Sebastian Bach, translated from the German of Philipp Spitta by Clara Bell and J. A. Fuller-Maitland. Novello & Co. 3 vols.
> An immense, involved, but fascinating work.

J. S. Bach, by Albert Schweitzer, translated by Ernest Newman. A. & C. Black. 2 vols.
> A beautiful and illuminating book.

Johann Sebastian Bach : the Story of the Development of A Great Personality, by Sir Hubert Parry. Putnam.
> A delightful study of Bach as a musician.

Johann Sebastian Bach : His Life, Art, and Work, by J. N. Forkel, translated and edited by C. Sanford Terry.
> The earliest Life of Bach.

Bach's Orchestra, by C. Sanford Terry. Oxford University Press.
> Full of value and interest to the student.

Bach : the Historical Approach, by C. Sanford Terry. Oxford University Press.
> Delightful and unusual essays on Bach.

The Music of Bach : an Introduction, by C. Sanford Terry. Oxford University Press.
> An admirable guide in small compass.

Johann Sebastian Bach the Organist, by A. Pirro. Translated by Wallace Goodrich. G. Schirmer.
> Illuminating.

The Organ Works of Bach, by Harvey Grace. Novello.
Clear, enthusiastic, and helpful.

Fugitive Notes on Some Cantatas and the Motets of J. S. Bach, by W. G. Whittaker. Oxford University Press.
Interesting and excellent.

In the " Musical Pilgrim " Series (Oxford University Press) there are the following books devoted to Bach :

C. Sanford Terry :
Mass in B Minor.
The Passions (2 vols.).
The Cantatas and Oratorios (2 vols.).
The Magnificat and Motets.

J. A. Fuller-Maitland :
The Keyboard Suites.
Brandenburg Concertos.
The 48 (2 vols.).

This is only a selection from the books on Bach in English.

SELECT LIST OF WORKS

ORGAN WORKS

All the following which are undated belong to the Weimar period 1708–17.

3 Preludes. A minor, C and G. (1700–8.)
3 Fugues. G minor, C and G minor.
4 Preludes and Fugues. A minor, C, C minor and E minor. (1700–8.)
9 Preludes and Fugues. A, A minor, C, C minor, D, F minor, G, G and G minor.
8 Short Preludes and Fugues.
3 Toccatas and Fugues. F, C and D minor.
2 Fantasias and Fugues, both in C minor.
Fantasia in C.
Pastorale in F.
Canzona in D minor.
Passacaglia in C minor.
A Little Book for the Organ. For beginners.
Fantasia and Fugue in G minor. (Hamburg, 1720.)
5 Preludes and Fugues. C, E minor, B minor, E flat ("St. Anne") and D minor. (1723 onwards.)
Toccata and Fugue in D minor ("Doric"). (1723.)
6 Sonatas. C, C minor, D minor, E flat, E minor and G. (1727.)
18 Choral Preludes. (Leipzig, 1749–50.)

KEYBOARD MUSIC

4 Fantasies. D, A minor, G minor and B minor.
4 Toccatas. E minor, D minor, G minor and G.
6 Fugues. A, A, A minor, A minor, A, B minor.
Prelude and Fugue. A minor.
Fugue. B flat, with theme on letters B.A.C.H. Possibly spurious.
All the above belong to the Weimar period, 1708–17.

Fantasia. C minor.
3 Fantasias and Fugues. D minor ("Chromatic"), B flat and D.
2 Toccatas. F sharp minor and C minor.
12 Little Preludes for beginners.

6 Little Preludes for beginners.

5 Fugues. C minor, C, C, D minor and D minor.

4 Preludes and Fugues. D minor, E minor, A minor, A minor.

3 Sonatas. A minor, C, D minor.

6 French Suites. B minor, C minor, D minor, E, E flat and G.

24 Preludes and Fugues—the "Well Tempered Clavier," vol. 1. All keys, major and minor. (1722.)

All the above belong to the Cöthen period, 1717–23.

2 Fantasias and Fugues. A minor and C minor.

4 Duets.

6 English Suites. A, A minor, D minor, E minor, F and G minor.

6 Partitas. A minor, B flat, C minor, D, E minor and G. Air with Thirty Variations ("Goldberg").

24 Preludes and Fugues—the "Well Tempered Clavier," vol. 2. All keys, major and minor. (1744.)
"Italian" Concerto. F major. (1735.)

All the above belong to the Leipzig period.

CHAMBER MUSIC

6 Sonatas for harpsichord and flute. C, E, E minor, A, B minor and E flat. (1717–23.)

8 Sonatas for harpsichord and violin. E minor, G, A, B minor, C minor, E, F minor and G. (1717–23.)

3 Sonatas for harpsichord and viola. D, G and G minor. (1717–23.)

6 Sonatas for solo violin. A minor, B minor, C, D minor ("Chaconne"), E, G minor. (1720.)

6 Sonatas for solo violincello. C, C minor, D, D minor, E flat and G. (1720.)

ORCHESTRAL MUSIC

6 Concertos for harpsichord. A, D, D minor, E, F minor and G minor. (1729–36.)

2 Concertos for two harpsichords. C minor and C. (1727–36.)

2 Concertos for three harpsichords. C and D minor. (1733.)
Concerto for four harpsichords. A minor (arr. from Vivaldi). (1733.)

2 Concertos for violin. A minor and E. (1717–23.)
Concerto for two violins. D minor. (1717–23.)

6 "Brandenburg" Concertos for various combinations of instruments. F, F, G, G, D and B flat.

4 Suites for various combinations of instruments. C, B minor, D and D.

SECULAR CANTATAS

The Contest of Phoebus and Pan. (Leipzig, 1731.)

The Coffee Cantata. (Leipzig, 1732.)
The Peasant Cantata. (Leipzig, 1742.)

CHURCH CANTATAS

Bach wrote well over 200 church cantatas, mostly at Leipzig in the years from 1723 onwards, when he set himself to compose a complete cycle for five church years. English titles are given below, in alphabetical order, of those most commonly performed nowadays; the figure in brackets is the number of the cantata in the Bach-Gesellschaft Edition.

Bide With Us (6). (1736.)
Christ Lay in Death's Dark Prison (4). (1724.)
Come, Redeemer of Our Race (61). (1714.)
From Depths of Woe I Call on Thee (38). (1736–44.)
God Goeth Up (43). (1735.)
God So Loved the World (68). (1735.)
God's Time is the Best (106). (1707–8.)
Hold in Affection Jesus Christ (67). (1724–7.)
How Brightly Shines the Morning Star (1). (Date unknown.)
Jesus Sleeps, What Hope Remaineth? (81). (1724.)
Lord is a Sun and Shield, The (79). (1735.)
Lord is My Shepherd, The (112). (1731–2.)
My Spirit was in Heaviness (21). (1714.)
O Light Everlasting (34). (1740 or 1741.)
O Praise the Lord for all His Mercies (28). (1723–7.)
Praise Jehovah, all Ye People (51). (1731–2.)
Praise our God who Reigns in Heaven (11). (?1734.)
Rise O Soul, this Happy Morning (180). (1740.)
Sages of Sheba, The (65). (1724.)
Sleepers, Wake (140). (1731 or ?1742.)
Stronghold Sure, A (1730.)
Wailing, Crying, Mourning, Sighing (12). (1724.)
Watch Ye, Pray Ye (70). (1716.)

OTHER SACRED WORKS

Magnificat. (Leipzig, 1723.)
St. John Passion. (Leipzig, 1724.)
St. Matthew Passion. (Leipzig, 1729.)
Easter Oratorio. (Leipzig, 1736.)
Christmas Oratorio. (Leipzig, 1734.)
Praise Ye the Lord. Motet for four voices.
Now Thank We All Our God. Motet for five voices. (1734.)
Jesu, Priceless Treasure. Motet for five voices. (1723.)
Sing Ye to the Lord. Motet for Double Chorus. (1725.)
Be not Afraid. Motet for Double Chorus. (?1726.)
Mass in B minor. (Leipzig, 1738.)

MISCELLANEOUS

A Notebook for Anna Magdalena Bach. (1275)

A Musical Offering on a theme by Frederick the Great· (Berlin, 1747.)

The Art of Fugue. 15 Fugues and 4 Canons on a theme in D minor (Leipzig, 1749–50.)

Various orchestral arrangements of works by Vivaldi and other composers.